THE MONROE DOCTRINE WAS A right one—the policy was a right one, not because it would require to be enforced by arms, but because it was well-timed. It was the result of a sagacious discovery of the tendency of the age. It will prevail if you affirm it. It will equally prevail if you neglect to affirm it hereafter as you have refused to do heretofore. As a practical question, therefore, it has ceased to be. It is obsolete. You are already the great continental power of America. But does that content you? I trust it does not. You want the commerce of the world, which is the empire of the world. This is to be looked for, not on the American lakes, nor on the Atlantic coast, nor on the Caribbean sea, nor on the Mediterranean, nor on the Baltic, nor on the Atlantic ocean, but on the Pacific ocean, and its islands and continents. Be not over-confident. Disregard not France, and England, and Russia. Watch them with jealousy, and baffle their designs against you. But look for those great rivals where they are to be found—on those continents and seas in the East where the prize which you are contending with them for is to be found. Open up a highway through your country from New York to San Francisco. Put your domain under cultivation, and your 10,000 wheels of manufacture in motion. Multiply your ships, and send them forth to the East. The nation that draws most materials and provisions from the earth, and fabricates the most, and sells the most of productions and fabrics to foreign nations, must be, and will be, the great power of the earth.

WILLIAM H. SEWARD, January 26, 1853

A
DIFFERENT
FRONTIER

Lloyd C. Gardner was born in Delaware, Ohio, and studied at Ohio Wesleyan University and the University of Wisconsin. He is the author of *Economic Aspects of New Deal Diplomacy*, and is at present Associate Professor of History at Rutgers University.

A
DIFFERENT
FRONTIER

Selected Readings in the
Foundations of American
Economic Expansion

EDITED WITH AN INTRODUCTION BY

Lloyd C. Gardner

CHICAGO   QUADRANGLE BOOKS   1966

Grateful acknowledgment is made to Harper & Row, Inc., for permission to reprint selections from *The Public Papers of Woodrow Wilson;* to Yale University Press for permission to reprint selections from *Earth Hunger and Other Essays* by William Graham Sumner; and to Charles Scribner's Sons for permission to reprint selections from *American and English Studies* by Whitelaw Reid.

CONTENTS

INTRODUCTION

FROM THE first shouted "Remember the Maine!" down to the present moment, Americans have been continuously engaged in reinterpreting the causes underlying American imperialism at the end of the nineteenth century. At first most contemporary reporters simply affirmed what they thought was obvious: American imperialism rose out of the smoke over the charge up San Juan Hill and that spewing forth from Admiral George Dewey's big guns in Manila Harbor. World power, they said, had been violently thrust upon the United States as a result of the war with Spain. When this smoke cleared in the Antilles and in the Philippines, American innocence was gone—and in its place, burdening the American conscience, appeared colonial worries and responsibilities in Cuba, Puerto Rico, Hawaii, and in the far-off Philippine Islands; and this last was a place so remote and unknown that the President of the United States himself supposedly was not sure of its location within 2,000 miles.

In a few years, it was admitted that at least one internal factor could be identified and isolated as a contributing cause: Yellow Journalism. Historians became interested in the exhortations of eastern papers in the months before the outbreak of war in April, 1898. They concluded that sensation promoters had fired American emotions to a peak over the struggle for freedom in Cuba. Similarly identified were the pleas and publicity efforts of the exiled Cuban junta operating out of New York. That the administration did indeed feel this heat was beyond doubt. President William McKinley's friend and counselor, Marcus A. Hanna, had hoped that war with Spain could be avoided, and that diplomatic pressures would bring a solution of the Cuban crisis short of armed conflict; but like many other political leaders then as now, Hanna recognized the impact the jingo press was having upon the country at large. He feared as well the determined missionary zeal of many American Protestant clergymen and laymen who felt called to the task of saving Cubans, Puerto Ricans, and Filipinos from superstition and all the dark forces they saw in European Catholicism. The vehemence of these Christian soldiers alarmed the less militant Hanna, and he gave full credit to their influence on decisions in the days before the declaration of war. But, among other gaps, this interpretation of events did not account for the annexation of Hawaii and was not relevant to the growing American economic drive into Canada and Central America.

A far longer step toward a comprehensive interpretation of American expansion came with the stress later writers placed upon an overpowering concept that described the American sense of mission in its broadest term: Manifest Destiny. This new understanding had the great advantage that it opened up the discussion and took it out from under those really very few smoke puffs covering the war months that summer of 1898. Manifest Destiny easily absorbed them into an overview which explained as well the emotions and ideas that had led to war with Mexico in 1846, and even reached back as far as the war with England in 1812. Some exponents of this view argued that all American history might be understood as the working out of this fateful Manifest Destiny. Standing at its beginning was the pioneer Puritan describing himself in essentially the same "chosen people" fashion as Mark Hanna's dedicated souls of the 1890's. And inherent in both instances was an assertive cultural justification for expansion over less endowed races.

In its best explications and expositions, such as Albert K. Weinberg's *Manifest Destiny,* this interpretation has very properly influenced all later writing on American expansion. On the other hand, early attempts to explain the Spanish-American War as the result of direct economic pressures on the business-oriented McKinley Administration did not succeed, in part because of their narrowness as opposed to the broader interpretations advanced by Weinberg and, more recently, by Richard W. Van Alstyne in his incisive look at all of American expansion, *The Rising American Empire.* Yet while it was well established by Julius W. Pratt, in *The Expansionists of 1898,* that important segments of the business community, far from desiring war, feared it would disrupt and even destroy the foundations then being constructed to bring the economy out of the lingering depression which began with the Panic of 1893, it is now known that other business leaders, if not actually in favor of the war, at least preferred it to the prolonged uncertainty which hung like a dark cloud over recovery prospects. But a more important consideration to remember is that the war was an incidental question (albeit a highly significant one) in its relation to the general matter of expansion of Asian and Latin American markets. Nearly all businessmen favored that aspiration, either as a general proposition, or in very specific terms concerning their own exports. Possession of Cuba and the Philippines would help to open the way for American goods, these men believed, but even without them other *entrepôts* would be found.

Moreover, very recently students of this period have pointed out that many Americans, intellectual leaders as well as political spokesmen and businessmen, did come to feel in the context of the 1890's, including the impact of this depression, that an expansion of their marketplace was necessary, indeed imperative, if the country were to fulfill its mission—its Manifest Destiny.

With the heightened efficiency of the American farm and factory, which allowed greater production at lower cost as their starting point, men who made this analysis were both optimistic and pessimistic about the future. Those who were optimistic pointed to American ability to sell goods in any market; those who remained pessimistic noted the uncertainties of the foreign outlets and the alternating dangers of the business cycle.

Charles S. Campbell's *Special Business Interests and the Open Door Policy*, William Appleman Williams' *The Tragedy of American Diplomacy*, and Walter LaFeber's *The New Empire*, all suggest that we need to broaden our understanding of the debates in the 1890's between avowed imperialists and equally avowed anti-imperialists. It is now apparent that most anti-imperialists actually were only anti-colonialists and not anti-expansionists as well. Some, like William Graham Sumner, for example, insisted that colonialism actually got in the way of *laissez-faire* expansion; others believed that the administration had taken on burdens and responsibilities not needed to sustain marketplace expansion. Still others opposed it quite plainly in moral terms. But they all agreed fundamentally about the dilemma posed by formal colonialism: If Washington accepted dominion over new territory beyond its continental frontiers it would either have to rule over it in the same way

European capitals did, and thereby give up a not insignificant part of its ideological heritage (and continuing *raison d'être* as the last great hope for mankind); or it would have to allow the new territories a share in ruling not only themselves but the country, a less than happy prospect for those Southern expansionists who still shuddered at memories of Reconstruction after the Civil War and the rule of black man over white. And in the context of the growth of Jim Crowism, hardly touched by the outcries of liberal reformers, such a choice was politically impossible.

This left the first alternative; the anti-imperialists came down hard with the argument, led by William Jennings Bryan in the campaign of 1900, that to abandon the American Dream for this projected American empire would not only corrupt the country abroad, but even more important, would submerge the chance for reform at home by completing the entrenchment of vested interests, which supposedly stood behind the colonial policy. Yet Bryan himself, while perhaps skeptical of the claims of some of its adherents, did in fact support John Hay's open door policy in China in that same campaign.

Another group of recent writers has emphasized sociological phenomena in accounting for the domestic Progressive movement and the overlapping imperial drive which began with the war, a thesis that differs more in emphasis perhaps than in basic interpretation. Bryan's quest for reform at home and the American quest for world stature, in this view, were not really antithetical even though many personalities in the struggle were, and even though sectionalism played an important part in the campaign of 1900. The "Great Commoner" headed an essentially middle class crusade, with broad Populist fringes, but the imperialists, too, were mostly middle class citizens. Squeezed between the force of gigantic corporations and the upward thrust of immigrant-dominated lower class pressures, American expansion offered them a chance to reassert older values of self-reliance and independence.

Many upper-class Americans chose to retreat into caste sanctuaries, but others, like Theodore Roosevelt, determined that instead of being ground to dust in the mills of industrial capitalism, they would seek out the sources of power and control the system from the top. Offshoot of an old agrarian-aristocratic lineage, and imbued with a deep sense of *noblesse oblige,* Roosevelt typified the virtues of the frontier—self-reliance, virility, and independence. Not concerned with personal money-making, McKinley's successor followed a foreign policy which he hoped would win the United States a prominent place among world powers. Certainly Howard K. Beale's *Theodore Roosevelt and America's Rise to World Power* places great weight upon his protagonist's ambitious drive to exercise power in world affairs and lends itself to such a sociological-psychological interpretation of this era.

There can be little doubt but that Theodore Roosevelt could have risen to prominence in any governmental system and that he simply adapted himself to the needs of his environment, whatever they might be. Timid capitalists annoyed and even angered him both before the Spanish-American War and after that conflict when they opposed his colonial or naval policies. The Adams brothers, Henry and Brooks, of Quincy, Massachusetts, have also provided an especially interesting study of the variant responses of the old upper class to the problems at the end of the nineteenth century. Sons of a presidential candidate, grandsons of a president, and great-grandsons of a Founding Father who became the second president of the United States, these two reacted in nearly opposite ways to the changes in their society. Henry, until very recently the better known by far, turned away and set his mind to work on the sources of power in earlier eras. He recorded in his autobiography that his world had centered on the values of eighteenth-century Harvard University and that these had all vanished from late nineteenth-century America.

But, although Brooks, too, had little use for the manners or morals of the new men of wealth, he sought the sources of power of his times —and of the future. He, too, studied the past, but to provide himself with an insight into the future. Deeply troubled by the Panic of 1893 and the depression which followed, Brooks wrote up his findings in *The Law of Civilization and Decay,* a gloomy book, which disturbed at least one reviewer, the normally optimistic Theodore Roosevelt. But with the Spanish-American War over, Brooks Adams, like his social peer John Hay, who was soon to be Secretary of State, believed that it had been a splendid little war, primarily because it had reinfused the economically dominated, lethargic American character with a dose of badly needed barbarian spirit. Economic-minded men had been stirred into a militant mood necessary to successful competition in the world's great market outlets and that, Adams thought, was well worth what it had cost.

Adams thereafter became a leading theorist of American imperialism, but with a small *i*, for his emphasis was always on economic expansion, not on land grabbing. Accepting wholeheartedly the system, with its tendency to concentration, he believed that a vent had to be found for overproduction so that the country might prosper without panics and depressions. Brooks's articles reached a wide range of policymakers as well as the educated public, and his private advice to Theodore Roosevelt and John Hay helped to establish an intellectual rationale for marketplace expansion and offered recommendations for carrying it out.

Like Brooks Adams, other imperial theoreticians such as Captain Alfred Thayer Mahan educated American political leaders to the needs of modern navies and commercial fleets, and especially to the role of stepping-stones or coaling stations; but a little-remembered State Department official, Frederic Emory, also reached a large audience with his frequent articles in well-known periodicals. Emory headed the Bureau of Foreign Commerce in the Department of State for several years beginning in January, 1898. Describing the mood of that decade, he wrote in 1902: "Although we were far from having occupied all our territory, in the sense of reducing it to tillage, and still had plenty of elbow room in the West, we were suffering from a sense of constraint, a vague feeling that we were not exerting ourselves to the full extent of our powers. For a long time we had been in the habit of regarding ourselves as a great people, but we felt that we were doing but little to impress this fact upon the rest of the world."

Fully as up to date as the most recent interpretations of American expansion, this statement and Emory's other writings did not try to separate out motives but attempted to sum them up in an outlook which saw the economic and political needs for imperialism developing out of the moods and ideas of the times. But Emory's daily work in the State Department, overseeing the editing and distribution of consular trade reports, led him to many of the same conclusions about the need for expansion of the American marketplace that characterized Adams's writings following the war with Spain. Emory had no difficulty in seeing the interchange between ideas and needs and the foreign policy their interactions produced.

The postulates of a better-known theoretician and historian, Frederick Jackson Turner, concerning the role of the frontier in molding the character of American society, had received a wide hearing somewhat earlier. It was in 1893 that the Wisconsin professor had delivered his paper on "The Significance of the Frontier in American History." His influence on Theodore Roosevelt and Professor Woodrow Wilson was readily affirmed by both men in the years following that paper's original publication, and it brought him recognition almost immediately. In 1896 the editor of the *Atlantic Monthly* asked Turner to do a major article on the "Problem of the West." In effect the historian was being asked to explain radical movements like the Populists to conservative easterners who were beginning to feel that the West ought to be told to go in peace if it could not live under the gold standard. Let that section have free silver and the boy orator from Nebraska, if it must, but not as part of the United States.

Turner's article took up the challenge quite explicitly: The problem of the West was that there was no more West. But instead of a division of the country, he predicted that there would more likely be a period of imperial expansion under a popular national hero to reestablish new frontiers.

A pre-Turner Turnerite, Iowa Republican John A. Kasson, had spoken in the same vein fifteen years earlier. A transplanted easterner, Kasson played a significant role in several national administrations, headed the American delegation to the Berlin Conference on the Congo Basin in 1884, and during the McKinley years was that President's Reciprocity Commissioner. In an article in the *North American Review* in 1881, he had stated: "We are rapidly utilizing the whole of our continental territory. We must turn our eyes abroad, or they will soon look inward upon discontent."

When added up, such views do not isolate the causes of specific policy decisions, but they do suggest that an intellectual rationale for a new outburst of expansionism was not thrust upon the United States as the result of the splendid little war with Spain.

The bedeviling question for these men and other intellectual and political leaders was not really "whether to" but "how to" expand. For the first time the nation seemed about to be filled up, capable of producing more than it could consume, and plagued with its new immigration problems. Among the first to feel the constriction of closed frontiers (in the broad sense) were agricultural interests, from the cotton growers in the South through midwestern corn and beef producers to those in the great wheat-flour milling states. They all counted on foreign trade to redress the imbalances in the domestic market. It was not at all unusual for some Populist senators and representatives to speak in these terms. Some argued for the greatest emphasis upon home market conditions and the need to reform society. But others combined a concern for foreign expansion with an equal desire for genuine reform. They asserted that the two causes were inseparable: the powers of the central government had to be used to guarantee an effectively functioning industrial and agricultural plant, and this system needed an ever-growing market at home *and* abroad. Only in this way could the social mobility that had existed in the nation's youth be preserved; and only in this way could social injustices be minimized or eliminated.

Once again to these questions the Spanish-American War was at most an incidental consideration, although "how to" deal with the new territories did demand an immediate reckoning and thereby accelerated the development of American policy.

Such a reckoning might have evolved in one of several ways. The United States could have become a formal colonial power like European nations, even though this meant accepting the loss of its anti-colonial heritage. To a limited extent in Hawaii, the Philippines, and Puerto Rico the United States reluctantly accepted that scepter, though vowing to grant varying degrees of self-government to these peoples. In Cuba the administration and Congress sought to retain an ideological purity while controlling the political and economic destiny of the island republic. Unhappily, in the final analysis, this amounted to wielding the "Big Stick" on occasion, instead of ruling continually with the scepter.

Still, it is correct to say that America's colonial experiment remained a very limited one. The islands retained were valuable mainly as stepping-stones to a much more important objective. A perfect example was America's determination not to allow Samoa to fall under

European domination. Although the United States hardly desired territorial dominion, it believed that Samoa's importance as a coaling station justified the tripartite regime established there with England and Germany at the beginning of the 1890's.

By that decade nearly all the immediately valuable areas which had been open to European or American annexation had been absorbed into one of the empires. This new imperialism with its search for personal and national glory, raw materials, and markets had commenced around 1870. Within twenty-five years nearly all of Africa and Southeast Asia had been sliced up among them. Had there been no other reason, this fact alone blocked wholesale land-grabbing by a relative newcomer like the United States or Germany. Leaders in these two nations, which were to follow a remarkably similar course of development in the coming years, evidenced little inclination to enter a race where all the best prizes had been awarded. And at the beginning of this new period of empire-building, Secretary of State Hamilton Fish explained to an empire-minded United States President Grant that the nation could better serve its interests in Latin America through trade and financial control than by conquest or annexation. In the 1880's Secretary of State Frederick Frelinghuysen reaffirmed this thesis and pinpointed the need for American financial institutions to seek connections and branches in South America to bring economic stability there with a resultant growth of inter-American trade. This decade ended with Secretary James G. Blaine's dramatic efforts to recapture the Pan American spirit through reciprocity treaties and to reinforce it with a Pan American railroad. Both men became strong advocates of ship subsidies to open new trade routes and bring the United States out of its unhealthy dependence upon European merchant vessels.

Meanwhile, Germany appeased its "jingoes" by picking up segments of land from the African continent; but Prince Otto von Bismarck's aims at the Berlin Conference of 1884 closely paralleled those advanced by America's John Kasson. Neither wanted greater national dominion; each desired an "open door" into the new state for its trade and ideas. Belgium's King Leopold had proposed to establish in the African hinterland an international settlement or free state, with all European states guaranteeing its international status; and the Berlin Conference had been called to work out the details.

Of all colonial policies those most objected to by outsiders concerned the trade and concession preferences retained by the mother country. These preferences were, after all, a primary motivation for establishing colonies. What the "open door" policy advocates urged in 1884, on the other hand, was not an end to European domination in the Congo Basin, but a tacit agreement that some areas, by their nature, because of their great value, or for reasons of political strategy, should be placed under a kind of international trusteeship—no matter how loosely defined. A measure of opportunity should be offered to members of the advanced industrial brotherhood. Friction between the brothers, increasing in 1884 and inevitable when all the best places were seized, might well be lessened by such understandings.

From the Congo Conference to the Sino-Japanese War was only a decade, but in those ten years American foreign policy was maturing along with the country. When Kasson brought back to the United States the proposed Congo Convention for American ratification, a change to Democratic party control of the national administration resulted in the agreement's being shelved. In 1895, however, Japan's military successes over the Celestial Empire of China and the favorable concessions exacted in the peace treaty ending Tokyo's "splendid little war" suddenly drew attention to new opportunities for colonial exploitation—and to fresh danger of colonial rivalry. After forcing Japan to surrender its major concessions, several European powers engaged themselves in fencing off "spheres of influence" throughout China. The sudden danger of 400 million Chinese disappearing into European and Japanese spheres of influence provided American policy-makers with their greatest challenge of the era: In 1896 Russia moved to protect its great investment in the Trans-Siberian Railroad and to extend its power over northern Manchuria. France and Great Britain solidified their holds in Yunnan and the Yangtze Valley; and in 1898, Germany took a terrible vengeance for the murder of two Christian missionaries by demanding almost complete control over the Shantung Peninsula.

To United States leaders China was an entirely different matter than Africa and the Congo Basin. In its early history the new republic had looked to Chinese markets when European mercantile laws shut it out of their empires. Even Kasson admitted that America's interest in the

Congo was mainly one of the future, while interest in China had begun early and had continued throughout the nineteenth century. The United States had always pursued an "open door" policy in the Far East; its ships had opened up Japan to the Western world in the 1850's; after the Civil War it had made a premature effort to do the same for the Hermit Kingdom of Korea.

Consequently, no matter what nation or person first whispered into State Department ears that Washington should take an immediate stand for equality of commercial opportunity in those Chinese ports located within the so-called "spheres of influence," or see Russia, Germany, France, and Japan erect impenetrable barriers around them, the first open-door note of 1899 bore the imprint of traditional American policy and interests. Secretary of State John Hay had been aware of similar British concern for Chinese survival as a single entity since his ambassadorship to that country just before assuming control of American foreign affairs; but the pressure exerted by domestic forces fashioned that message and determined the nature of Washington's second open-door note of 1900.

In the first circular, Hay asked the powers to accept in principle the idea of equality of opportunity in ports and areas under their immediate influence. Yet no sooner had the replies been received in Washington, some of which were obviously evasive, than the Boxer Rebellion against all foreigners erupted in June, 1900. This raised the disquieting possibility that the real answer to the Chinese question would become a military one. No doubt armed intervention would be followed by armed conquest; China's future then would belong to those Europeans who followed their armies into the subdued cities, no matter what lip service might be paid to the idea of Chinese sovereignty.

Not at all by luck, the United States had retained the Philippine Islands and, as Whitelaw Reid and others had predicted, this base gave Washington a chance to send troops to participate in the suppression of the Boxers. Once in China, American commanders stood as far apart from their allies as possible, and championed the maintenance of Chinese territorial and administrative integrity. Meanwhile, in Washington the State Department readied and dispatched a second note on China which called upon the powers not to take advantage of the rebellion to destroy that integrity, and to join the United States in safe-guarding "for the world, the principle of equal and impartial trade with all parts of the Chinese Empire."

This Chinese policy went far beyond what Kasson had wanted the United States to do in the Congo. From the outset the chances for the success of the "open door" policy in China teetered upon a series of unlikely balances. The most delicate balance concerned the continued political relationships of the European powers and their alliances. Changes in those relationships might militate against American policy in China, or, more optimistically, could advance its aims. Chinese ability to strengthen its grip on outlying provinces on the borders of the Celestial Empire was another problematical factor. If Peking should accomplish this and achieve a strong central government, temptations to separate such provinces would diminish. China's reliance upon a policy formulated by outside interests, however, no matter how friendly, was hardly a favorable situation. Finally, there was a third consideration which troubled Washington policy-makers: There was no assurance that a change in administrations might not bring to power leaders who would give it all up as a bad proposition which over-extended American commitments.

Late in his career, Secretary Hay wrote to a friend that the United States had to hold on to the open-door policy like grim death, but even he was doubtful if the country would risk a military conflict to main-tain the integrity of China. At the same time, one goal of the open-door policy at the time of both the Congo Convention and the Boxer Rebellion was to reduce the chances of just such a conflict. Moreover, in 1903 the United States attempted to aid China's internal fiscal situation in what might be called the beginning of dollar diplomacy. Although unsuccessful, American policy-makers continued to make such attempts to strengthen Chinese nationality.

Encouraging also to American leaders was a continuing expansion of their export trade in Europe and elsewhere, which spurred some businessmen and writers to speak proudly of an American "Commer-cial Invasion" of Europe. This both strengthened the basis for the open-door policy and assured a sustained interest in advancing it. In fact, in the next few years it became a generalized approach to colonial areas and reached a peak with American attempts to write it into the League of Nations Mandate System.

Theodore Roosevelt once even equated the open-door policy in China with the Monroe Doctrine in Latin America. That opinion he advanced in 1901 before assuming the presidency; he modified it, however, as American domination in the Caribbean and in Central America, and his own corollary to the Monroe Doctrine, led to much closer control than an open-door policy would permit.

But Roosevelt's Far Eastern policy further committed the United States to the open-door policy for China. In agreeing to mediate between Russia and Japan after the two had joined battle, he exacted a series of pledges from the victorious Japanese that they would honor their word to maintain equal opportunity. Then he built the Great White Fleet to back up his demands.

In the years leading up to the Russo-Japanese War after the Boxer Rebellion, the greatest threat to Mr. Hay's policy was assumed to be Russian forward movements in Manchuria. Even more alarmed were the Japanese who needed only assurance from some major European power against combined opposition before bringing the situation to a showdown. That assurance they gained in the formal Anglo-Japanese alliance of 1902.

For the United States the Russo-Japanese War was an unexpected *deus ex machina* which gave American diplomacy a chance to restore the balance of power in the Far East, a task that Theodore Roosevelt undertook with verve and determination. Unfortunately, it was a *deus ex machina* that failed: Japan's Manchurian policy soon proved equally unwelcome to American policy-makers. In an effort to reach a *modus vivendi* in the Far East, Washington and Tokyo undertook negotiations in the following years which led to several bilateral agreements and understandings, none of which really brought their conflict nearer to solution. Each one did, nevertheless, deepen the American commitment to its China policy for good or ill.

Non-colonial in theory and practice, the open-door policy could be asserted by a nation like the United States because of its steadily increasing efficiency and ability to compete in the world market with any nation, so long as there was equality of opportunity. Moreover, because it called for no imperial responsibilities and obligations, this policy allowed the United States to maintain the illusion that it was still isolated and free from entangling alliances. Called into being by an interaction of American ideas and interests, the open-door policy climaxed the specific developments of more than two decades and answered the challenge so forcefully posed by William H. Seward on January 26, 1853.

The selections that follow are divided into three broad sections: In the first, discussion of the transformation in American expansionism or Manifest Destiny after the Civil War is followed by readings on the conditions and events of the 1880's and 1890's leading to the outburst of imperialism in 1898; in the second, various political and intellectual leaders debate the "how to" of American expansionism; and in the third, they consider the problems created by the new position of the United States in world affairs.

I
The New
Manifest Destiny

ALTHOUGH Secretary of State William H. Seward had badly wanted Alaska from the Russians in order to project a territorial base well out into the Pacific Ocean where, he predicted, the great rivalries of the future would surface, Republican foreign policy under his guidance had turned its back on the land-grabbing schemes of the 1850's. In those years the newly organized Republicans campaigned hard against such unhealthy expansionism, linking it to the slave interests in particular and to the Democratic party in general. As long as the nation remained agitated over the future of Cuba or excited by the exploits of various adventurers in their filibustering campaigns in Central America, the settlement of the basic social question at home was delayed. Climaxing their determination, once they achieved power, not to tolerate such circumventions was Abraham Lincoln's flat rejection of the compromise proposal to draw an imaginary line from coast to coast separating slave states from free. No more than a year or so would go by, replied Lincoln, than the South would revive its arguments for Cuban annexation. And with that determination not to allow such an opportunity to the slave states, the first Republican President faced directly into a civil war crisis.

But after Ulysses S. Grant moved from the final triumph of that war at Appomattox, Virginia, to an easier victory in the national election of 1868, his newly acquired interest in the fate of Caribbean islands like Santo Domingo, as well as Cuba, encouraged those who hoped to see the old American Manifest Destiny on the march once again. This alarmed not only the Radical Republicans, but also Grant's moderate

Secretary of State, Hamilton Fish. Like his fellow New Yorker Seward, Fish had a vision of a new Manifest Destiny arising out of the continuing expansion of American foreign commerce.

The Secretary's chance to explain these views came when he wrote an answer to President Grant's questions about the state of American trade with Latin America. In his "Circular" of July 14, 1870, Secretary Fish set forth a proposed Latin American policy as well as a reasoned answer to the President's queries. Not unnaturally Fish began by recalling the Monroe Doctrine and the diplomacy of its principal author, John Quincy Adams, paying special attention and respect to that President's hopes for the Pan American Conference of 1826. Those hopes for closer political and commercial ties broke on the rock of African slavery, insisted Fish, when a Congress influenced by slave interests failed to support Adams. Now, at last, rejoiced Grant's Secretary of State, that crippling influence had been eliminated and the country could retrieve its mistakes.

Fish's 1870 Circular also bespoke a changing attitude which many American leaders would eventually take toward Latin American revolutions. His concern for stability and peaceful development, as safeguards against foreign annexationist plots and interventions, was expressed in the latter part of this state paper and rounded out his ideas about the Western Hemisphere.

John A. Kasson, Iowa politician and rising foreign policy spokesman, picked up Fish's thesis some eleven years later and drew from it additional conclusions: The Monroe Doctrine badly needed updating to meet a challenge, not of territorial alienation, but of strong commercial nations in Europe which sought instead to control the marketplaces of Latin America for their surpluses. Calling for ship subsidies and an American developed canal across the narrow waist of Central America, he repeated a theme that became louder and more strident every year.

After serving as American Minister at Vienna, Kasson came to see a magnificent future for his nation's commerce in Africa as well. His efforts as Chief Delegate to the Berlin Conference of 1884, though personally disappointing for him in the end, showed a rising interest in the United States regarding the problem of colonial empires and their rivalries. American leaders were also concerned about developing inroads into the trade and concessions of such dependent areas.

Although a Republican president would no doubt have sent the Congo Convention on to the Senate for ratification, other matters did go forward regardless of the party in control, and public figures like Secretary of the Treasury Hugh McCulloch were thinking out loud about the tariff wall and concluding that unless a more flexible attitude were taken it might become a fence holding in unnaturally the "plethora of manufactured goods" which had helped to bring on an abrupt downturn in the economy in 1883 and 1884. Such fears appeared and receded with each turn of the business cycle all through these years.

The Benjamin Harrison Administration carried out several important policies designed to improve United States opportunities for world trade. Blaine's Pan Americanism would have pleased both Seward and Fish. This Administration also began the modernization of the navy and moved to secure an important naval station in the Pacific. With the Panic of 1893 and the depression that followed, tariff reformers received a setback when the Republicans ran William McKinley on a platform demanding more protection for the home market and the home workman.

Although overshadowed by this issue, pleas for tariff bargaining and selective reciprocity actually grew louder. An English writer, J. S. Jeans, foresaw the disturbing impact the search for markets would have upon the old world. His look at the "Labour War in the United States" offered a penetrating report on industrial conditions in America and concluded with a dark warning that the enlarging capacities and increasing efficiency of American factories would soon threaten England's industrial outlets in all the world's great selling areas.

Frederick Jackson Turner's discussion of the "Problem of the West" began with the premise that America was now nearing maturity as an industrial society, but he was more concerned with how the country would manage its "frontier" ideology, which was deeply ingrained in the society as a whole. He distrusted the argument of those who assumed that the conflict between the older West (now the settled East) and the more recent West would continue to divide the country. Instead, he predicted a search for new frontiers.

The two selections from Woodrow Wilson's early writings illustrate the influence Turner's postulates had upon the rising generation of intellectuals and political leaders. Wilson saw in 1889 that the century which stretched uncertainly before the republic would be harder and more complex than the first hundred years of the nation's life; in 1897 he was pondering Professor Turner's ideas in that relation. His further thoughts on these problems are reserved for a later section.

From agricultural and industrial leaders came statements and resolutions which plainly described their attitudes toward the needs of the times and the means to fulfill their desires. Several of these are presented as the final selections in this first chapter.

HAMILTON FISH, "Latin American Circular," July 14, 1870

The Secretary of State, to whom was referred the resolution of the Senate requesting the President "to institute an inquiry, by such means as in his judgment shall be deemed proper, into the present condition of the commercial relations between the United States and the Spanish-American states on this continent, and between those countries and other nations, and to communicate to the Senate full and complete statements regarding the same, together with such recommendations as he may think necessary to promote the development and increase of our commerce with those regions, and to secure to the United States that proportionate share of the trade of this continent to which their close relations of geographical contiguity and political friendship with all the states of America justly entitle them," has the honor to report:

The resolution justly regards the commercial and the political relations of the United States with the American states of Spanish origin as necessarily dependent upon each other. If the commerce of these countries has been diverted from its natural connection with the United States, the fact may probably be partly traced to political causes, which have been swept away by the great civil convulsion in this country.

For the just comprehension of the position of this government in the American political system, and for the causes which have failed to give it hitherto the influence to which it is properly entitled, by reason of its democratic system, and of the moderation and sense of justice which have distinguished its foreign policy through successive administrations from the birth of the nation until now, it is necessary to make a brief notice of such measures as affect our present relations to the other parts of this continent.

The United States were the first of the European colonies in America to arrive at maturity as a people, and assume the position of an independent republic. Since then important changes have taken place in various nations in every part of the world. Our own growth in power has been not the least remarkable of all the great events of modern history.

When at the conclusion of the revolutionary war, having conquered by arms our right to exist as a sovereign state, that right was at length recognized by treaties, we occupied only a narrow belt of land along the Atlantic coast, hemmed in at the north, the west, and the south by the possessions of European governments, or by uncultivated wastes beyond the Alleghenies, inhabited only by the aborigines. But, in the very infancy of the United States, far-sighted statesmen saw and predicted that, weak in population and apparently restricted in available territory as the new republic then was, it had within it the germs of colossal grandeur, and would, at no remote day, occupy the continent of America with its institutions, its authority, and its peaceful influence. . . .

The foreign policy of these early days was not a narrow one. During this period we secured the evacuation by Great Britain of the country wrongfully occupied by her on the lakes; we acquired Louisiana; we set the example of resisting and chastising the piracies of the Barbary States; we initiated in negotiations with Prussia the long line of treaties for the liberalization of war and the promotion of international intercourse; and we steadily demanded, and at length obtained, indemnification from various governments for the losses we had suffered by foreign spoliations in the wars of Europe.

To this point in our foreign policy we had arrived when the revolutionary movements in Spanish and Portuguese America compelled a modification of our relations with Europe, in consequence of the rise of new and independent states in America. . . .

A vast field was thus opened to the statesmen of the United States for the peaceful introduction, the spread, and the permanent establishment of the American ideas of republican government, of modification of the laws of war, of liberalization of commerce, of religious freedom and toleration, and of the emancipation of the New World from the dynastic and balance of power controversies of Europe.

Mr. John Quincy Adams, beyond any other statesmen of the time in this country, had the knowledge and experience, both European and American, the comprehension of thought and purpose, and the moral convictions which peculiarly fitted him to introduce our country into this new field, and to lay the foundation of an American policy. The declaration known as the Monroe Doctrine, and the objects and purposes of the Congress of Panama, both supposed to have been largely inspired by Mr. Adams, have influenced public events from that day to this, as a principle of government for this continent and its adjacent islands. . . .

This policy is not a policy of aggression; but it opposes the creation of European dominion on American soil, or its transfer to other European powers, and it looks hopefully to the time when, by the voluntary departure of European governments from this continent and the adjacent islands, America shall be wholly American.

It does not contemplate forcible intervention in any legitimate contest; but it protests against permitting such a contest to result in the increase of European power or influence; and it ever impels this government, as in the late contest between the South American republics and Spain, to interpose its good offices to secure an honorable peace.

The Congress of Panama was planned by Bolivar to secure the union of Spanish America against Spain. It had originally military as well as political purposes. In the military objects the United States could take no part; and indeed the necessity for such objects ceased when the full effects of Mr. Monroe's declarations were felt. But the pacific objects of the congress, the establishment of close and cordial relations of amity, the creation of commercial intercourse, of interchange of political thought, and of habits of good understanding between the new republics and the United States and their respective citizens, might perhaps have been attained had the administration of that day received the united support of the country. Unhappily they were lost; the new states were removed from the sympathetic and protecting influence of our example, and their commerce, which we might then have secured, passed into other hands, unfriendly to the United States.

In looking back upon the Panama Congress from this length of time, it is easy to understand why the earnest and patriotic men who endeavored to crystallize an American system for this continent failed.

Mr. Clay and Mr. Adams were far-sighted statesmen, but unfortunately they struck against the rock of African slavery. One of the questions proposed for discussion in the conference was, "The consideration of the means to be adopted for the entire abolition of the African slave trade," to which proposition the committee of the United States Senate of that day replied, "The United States have not certainly the right, and ought never to feel the inclination, to dictate to others who may differ with them upon this subject, nor do the committee see the expediency of insulting other states with whom we are maintaining relations of perfect amity, by ascending the moral chair, and proclaiming from thence mere abstract principles, of the rectitude of which each nation enjoys the perfect right of deciding for itself. . . .

Thus the necessity at that day of preserving the great interest of the Southern States in African slavery, and of preventing a change in the character of labor in the islands of Cuba and Porto Rico, lost to the United States the opportunity of giving a permanent direction to the political and commercial connections of the newly enfranchised Spanish-American states, and their trade passed into hands unfriendly to the United States, and has remained there ever since.

Events, subsequent to that date, have tended to place us in a position to retrieve our mistakes; among which the events may be particularly named the suppression of the rebellion, the manifestation of our undeveloped and unexpected military power, the retirement of the French from Mexico, and the abolition of slavery in the United States.

There is good reason to believe that the latter fact has had an important influence in our favor in Spanish America. It has caused us to be regarded there with more sympathetic as well as more respectful consideration; it has relieved those republics from the fear of filibusterism, which had been formerly incited against Central America and Mexico in the interest of slave extension; and it has produced an impression of the stability of our institutions and of our public strength sufficient to dissipate the fears of our friends and the hopes of those who wish us ill. . . .

It will not be presumptuous after the foregoing sketch to say, with entire consideration for the sovereignty and national pride of the Spanish-American republics, that the United States, by the priority of their independence, by the stability of their institutions, by the regard of their people for the forms of law, by their resources as a government, by their naval power, by their commercial enterprise, by the attractions which they offer to European immigration, by the prodigious internal development of their resources and wealth, and by the intellectual life of their population, occupy of necessity a prominent position on this continent, which they neither can nor should abdicate, which entitles them to a leading voice, and which imposes on them duties of right and of honor regarding American questions, whether those questions affect emancipated colonies, or colonies still subject to European domination. . . .

With the Spanish islands of Cuba and Porto Rico we maintain, in spite of their adverse legislation, a large commerce by reason of our necessities and their proximity. In the year ending June 30, 1869, we imported from them merchandise valued at $65,609,274. During the same period we sent them goods to the value only of $15,313,919.

The prohibitory duties forced upon them by the policy of Spain shut out much that we might supply. Their tropical productions, for instance, are too valuable to allow their lands to be given up to the growth of breadstuffs; yet, instead of taking these articles from the superabundant fields of their nearest neighbors, they are forced to go to the distant plains of Spain. It will be for the interest of the United States to shape its general policy so that this relation of imports and exports shall be altered in Cuba when peace is restored and its political condition is satisfactorily established.

With none of the other Spanish-American states in North and South America are our commercial relations what they should be. Our total imports in the year ending June 30, 1869, from these countries were less than $25,000,000 (or not one-half the amount from Cuba alone), and our exports for the same time to them were only $17,-850,313; and yet these countries have an aggregate population nearly or quite as great as that of the United States; they have republican forms of government, and they profess to be, and probably really are, in political sympathy with us.

This Department is not able to give with entire accuracy the imports and exports of Great Britain with the same countries during the corresponding period. It is believed, however, the following figures will be found to be not far from correct:

Imports to Great Britain, $42,820,942; exports from Great Britain, $40,682,102.

It thus appears that notwithstanding the greater distance which the commerce has to travel in coming to and from Great Britain, notwithstanding the political sympathy which ought naturally to exist between republics, notwithstanding the American idea which has been so prominently and so constantly put forward by the Government of the United States, notwithstanding the acknowledged skill of American manufactures, notwithstanding the ready markets which the great cities of the United States afford for the consumption of tropical productions, the inhabitants of the Spanish-American continent consume of the products of Great Britain more than twice the quantity they take of the products of the United States, and that they sell to us only three-fifths of the amount they sell to Great Britain. . . .

That their commerce with the United States is not large, may be partially explained by the fact that these states have been subject to many successive revolutions since the failure of the Congress of Panama. These revolutions not only exhaust their resources and burden them with debt, but they check emigration, prevent the flow of foreign capital into the country, and stop the enterprise which needs a stable government for its development.

These suggestions are, however, applicable to the British commerce as well as to our own, and they do not explain why we, with the natural advantages in our favor, fall so far behind. The Isthmus of Panama is the common point where the commerce of the western coasts of Mexico and South America meets. When it arrives there, why should it seek Liverpool and London rather than New York?

The political causes which have operated to divert this commerce from us the Secretary of State has endeavored to explain. A favorable time has now come for removing them—for laying the foundation of an American policy which shall bind us in closer union with the American republics. Let them understand that the United States do not covet their territories; that our only desire is to see them peaceful, with free and stable governments, increasing in wealth and population, and developing in the lines which their own traditions, customs, habits, laws, and modes of thought will naturally take them. Let them feel that, as in 1826 so now, this government is ready to aid them to the full extent of its constitutional power in any steps which they may take for their better protection against anarchy. Let them be convinced that the United States are prepared, in good faith and without ulterior purposes, to join them in the development of a peaceful American commercial policy, that may in time include this continent and the West Indian Islands. Let this be comprehended, and there will be no political reason why we may not "secure to the United States that proportionate share of the trade of this continent to which their close relations of geographical contiguity and political friendship with all the states of America justly entitle them."

(From *Papers Relating to the Foreign Relations of the United States, 1870,* Washington, 1871, pp. 254-261)

JOHN A. KASSON, "The Monroe Doctrine in 1881," 1881

It is no longer for us a question of despotism extending its sphere of supremacy to America. It is a question now of commercial rivalry and commercial advantages. Covetous eyes are cast on outlying islands and continental coasts of Central and South America. A steam-ship line is preferred to an army; a canal to a fortification; a good harbor to a strong citadel. One far-sighted government, eager for the extension of its foreign trade and naval influence, has initiated negotiations for the transfer to it of a seemingly unimportant but really commanding tract of waste land. The weak government approached may be disposed to yield. The islands of the Central, the Pacific, and the Southern seas have become objects of special interest and examination to more than one of the naval and commercial powers of the Old World. At least two of the Continental powers have been looking diligently for new colonial stations across or in the world of Western waters. The unhappy and repeated dissensions and irregularities of the Central and South American states furnish too many occasions for foreign interference and foreign claims of indemnity. Their resulting financial condition offers too strong temptation to relieve embarrassments by the expropriation of territorial rights and privileges. It is easy to find occasion for a naval war, if any European power desires a pretext for the seizure of a port or territory. The recognized doctrine of a war indemnity stands in aid of the acquisitive purpose. . . .

Let us revive the doctrine, not the declaration, of President Monroe's administration, in the light of later experience and of wider development of interests. The time is most favorable. Our foreign relations are universally amicable. Our domestic prosperity and contentment frees the Government from anxious interior cares. Our finances are well ordered and satisfactory. We can freely turn our eyes abroad, not for aggressive action, but for peaceful and secure development. We can tranquilly determine our policy upon the questions under review, and inquire whether we ought not to advance from the earlier declaration, made by the President sixty years ago, when we had no Pacific coast, to a position and to action more conformable to our present condition and interests, and to the present ambitions of other governments. For our own territory, or for our political system—defended by 50 millions of people devoted to it, and ready to spring to arms for its defense—we fear nothing. The sentiment of monarchy toward popular republics has radically changed. Liberty has advanced eastward with long strides, while despotism has receded to the borders of Asia. History, authority, reason, and existing conditions amply justify the formal declaration of the principle foreshadowed by Mr. Monroe's advisers. The United States could not witness with indifference the establishment on these American continents of any new military or naval position, in whatever way acquired, or of any new colony under European jurisdiction, or the transfer to any other European naval power of any existing colonial dependency.

It would not be proper to disclose here all the reasons which urge us to the early and resolute adoption of this principle, and to the preparation of all needful means for its enforcement. If not now formulated and declared, it should be accepted by our statesmen, not as a topic for academical discussion or stump oratory, but as a basis for firm and decisive action, and in full view of its possible consequences. None but the stupid can have failed to observe, in the history of British-American relations, a singular alternation of equitable and aggressive dispositions toward the interests of the United States—the latter, unfortunately, manifested in times of our trouble or weakness. Germany and France are strong rival commercial and aggressive powers. Both are seeking outlying positions of future advantage for commercial and military purposes. He is greatly mistaken who supposes that the rejection of the imperial dynasty by France has changed in this respect the spirit of the French governing classes. . . .

How much longer is our unobservant Congress to shut its eyes to the sagacious extension of the commercial lines and positions of foreign countries? How much longer are we to continue blind to the demands for new markets for our already excessive and rapidly increasing production? How much longer fail to seize opportunities for the wider distribution of our manufactures? If we have no oceanic lines under our flag leading to and by the positions which European governments covet, with what argument shall we meet them when they seek to establish themselves there? They may say to us: "Certainly, you entertain a sentiment that you have, or ought to have, a greater interest than we possess in these places; but we show you our flag there, our steamers, our traders,—where are yours?"

Let us implore Congress and the Executive to release themselves, in part, from interior political struggles, and to remember that it is the duty of statesmanship to anticipate the future. The farmer and manufacturer plant before reaping their profit. The United States have hitherto, for many years, refused to plant at all. One million dollars saved from ineffectual interior improvements, or added to that expenditure, if their importance is insisted upon, will open several new lines and markets to our agriculture and manufactures. Without it, our surplus will soon roll back from the Atlantic coast upon the interior, and the wheels of prosperity will be clogged by the very richness of the burden which they carry, but cannot deliver. Without it, European interests will seize and monopolize the points of greatest future importance to our safety and our commercial welfare. There are islands, and bays, and ports, and lines of communication which it may yet cost us a war to save to our interests, but which could now be peacefully saved. The tradition against the policy of outlying possessions is, at this stage of our history, simply imbecile. It belongs to a country of few resources, timid and trembling in the presence of some great naval power. We have passed that stage of our existence. We are rapidly utilizing the whole of our continental territory. We must turn our eyes abroad, or they will soon look inward upon discontent. Touching the two great oceans which divide the world, this republic should, like the Roman Janus, have two faces, regarding both Europe and Asia, and the islands interposed. It is the duty, alike of her political interests and her wealth, to connect the waters of the two seas which embrace her coasts, and then to keep the connecting waters bright with her passing keels. The Spanish nations of this hemisphere are still hardly opened to the enterprise of our people. For the most part they can only be reached under a foreign flag, though the United States were the first to recognize their independence, to aid their development, and to defend their rights under the menace of war. For 60 years we have asserted our special interest in this hemisphere. To-day what flag dominates in its harbors and along its coasts? The answer is humiliating. It calls for a change of our passive policy into one of action, knitting more and more closely our union with our sister republics, and opening wide the doors to the commercial activity of our people. Then shall we have irresistible arguments to sustain our non-colonization policy, and ample returns for our wise and beneficent enterprise.

(From *The North American Review*, December, 1881, CXXXIII, 523-533)

JOHN A. KASSON, "The Congo Conference and the President's Message," 1886

The conditions under which commerce should be conducted with Central Africa for all future time, and the securities to be afforded to the persons and institutions of Christian civilization established there, were deemed by fourteen foremost nations of the earth to be of sufficient importance to justify an international consultation on the subject. The resolutions of this assembly were believed by thirteen governments to be so useful as to merit approval. It seems that our Government, or rather its executive officer, holds them of so little importance as not to deserve the consideration of the American senate. So it appears by the following extract from the President's message:

"The action taken by this Government last year in being the first to recognize the flag of the International Association of the Congo has been followed by formal recognition of the new nationality which succeeds to its sovereign powers.

"A conference of delegates of the principal commercial nations was held at Berlin last winter to discuss methods whereby the Congo Basin might be kept open to the world's trade. Delegates attended on behalf of the United States on the understanding that their part should be merely deliberative, without imparting to the results any binding character, so far as the United States were concerned. This reserve was due to the indisposition of this Government to share in any disposal by an international congress of jurisdictional questions in remote foreign territories. The results of the conference were embodied in a formal act of the nature of an international convention, which laid down certain obligations purporting to be binding on the signatories, subject to ratification within one year. Notwithstanding the reservation under which the delegates of the United States attended, their signatures were attached to the general act in the same manner as those of the plenipotentiaries of other governments, *thus making the United States appear, without reserve or qualification, as signatories to a joint international engagement imposing on the signers the conservation of the territorial integrity of distant regions* where we have no established interests or control.

"This Government does not, however, regard its reservation of liberty of action in the premises as at all impaired; and holding that an engagement to share *in the obligation of enforcing neutrality in the remote valley of the Congo would be an alliance* whose responsibilities we are not in a position to assume, I abstain from asking the sanction of the senate to that general act."

Are these official observations justified? Or has the President been ill-advised, and his message made the vehicle of wholly erroneous statements?

A slight inquiry by the Secretary into diplomatic law, or into the text of the document, would have assured him that his implication that the United States delegates had surpassed their instructions in certifying by their signatures the final acts of the conference was wholly gratuitous. That signature did not make the United States appear as signatories "without reserve or qualification." Not only was the

reserve and qualification—that the whole was subject to approval by
the home government—contained in the acceptance of the invitation
itself, but it was embodied in the text of the final Act which provides
that it shall only take effect for each power when that power shall
have ratified it. . . .

But the more important questions relate to the conclusions themselves of the conference and their importance to American interests,
present and future. The President admits the need of regulated relations with that region by submitting recommendations for commercial
agencies there, and by having formally recognized its principal nationality, although it occupies only about one-third of the country
affected. With this nation, as with nearly all the rest of the region,
we have no diplomatic or consular arrangements or securities unless
those adopted by the conference are accepted. Certainly then it is
worth the trouble to inquire what the delegates of so many nations
did actually recommend for the common interest of all in their
future relations with one-third of a great continent.

A meeting of the principal governments of the world for the sole
purpose of promoting the peace of nations, the interests of international
commerce and the progress of Christian civilization is an event so
unusual that it deserves more than superficial attention. History records
many such meetings of powers in order to restrain or ratify warlike
aggressions, to regulate the balance of continental power, to define
political jurisdictions, or to divide the fruits of conquest. In late
years however, and at the primary invitation of the United States, they
have repeatedly assembled for the regulation of postal communications
between themselves, and for an agreement on scientific questions. An
examination of the record of the Berlin Conference of 1884 will
show a meeting on a still higher plane, suggested by the discoveries
of an American citizen, and by the political action of the United
States in recognizing a new-born State.

Within the last two decades travelers had forced their way up the
Nile, and from Mozambique westward, until the great lakes of Central
Africa and the thickly populated country around them had been discovered and partially explored, and a great river found whose destina-
tion and commercial utility were unknown. To the task of solving
this doubt an American devoted himself with rare sagacity, intrepidity,

and pluck. Undeterred by savage nature and more savage man, he, during 999 days, traversed a continent which had been dark during all historic ages, and displayed the flag of the newest great nation of time to the most unknown people of the earth. From a line less than 100 miles from the eastern coast of Africa, until he saw the rise and fall of the Atlantic tide in the Lower Congo, Stanley saw neither fortress, nor flag of any civilized nation, save that of the United States, which he carried along the arterial watercourse of a region inhabited by people estimated at more than 40 millions in number.

Thus was opened up a vast field for the operations of Christianity, of civilization, and of commerce. The American Government claimed nothing from the right of discovery. The enlightened King of the Belgians, mourning the loss of an only heir to his throne, resolved to dedicate a royal fortune to the founding of a free and progressive state in the newly discovered center of a populous continent. Routes were opened, stations established, officers appointed and the work begun. The first appeal for recognition and for moral support was naturally and justly made to the Government whose flag was first carried across the region. The President and Senate responded favorably to the appeal and recognized the occupation as lawful, being founded on treaties having the consent of the native authority, and promising equal and just treatment to all American interests.

But European commercial interests were also involved. European consent was needed. Europe embraced all the colonizing powers. Two of them were already pushing forward their colonial claims to this region. Both of these governments had, for generations, adopted the policy of colonial monopolies, excluding other commercial nations from access to their colonies except on terms of great inequality. Should this region fall under such control, not only the trade and influence of the country which claimed its discovery, but of all other non-occupying governments, would be practically excluded from its benefits. All these nations had a common interest in establishing there the liberty and equality of trade, and in the contribution of civilizing influences. The missionaries of the United States churches were there. Some American manufacturers were making their way there. Six millions of the African races now in America might yet contribute a useful emigration in aid of its civilization. We were already the principal consumers of one of its chief products. In much less time than our own Mississippi valley was opened and settled after discovery we might expect the opening up of a profitable trade with the Congo valley and the Lake region of Central Africa, if we could have free access to it from the east and west. The first steps are always doubtful, sluggish, and expensive. Later, modern nations march with rapidity and security. How should the United States and other non-possessory nations obtain their equal rights of intercourse with this vast region? How should they be treated among its present and rival occupants? And how should it be known which colonial power really and rightfully controlled the oceanic gateways to this region?

These comprehensive international questions presented themselves to the far-seeing mind of Germany's great statesman—not only Germany's but the world's foremost statesman. They must be settled before indefinite claims had crystallized into rights of unquestioned possession and before the old regime of colonial exclusiveness should be established never to be uprooted. France was already pushing her colonial adventures to the northern bank of the Congo. Portugal was claiming the south bank and indefinitely eastward, claiming indeed both banks by right of prior discovery of only the mouth of this great river. Other European powers were founding establishments and interests there.

The German Chancellor decided to invite a Conference of the commercial nations to consider the questions of, first: Liberty of trade in the Congo basin; second: Freedom of navigation in the Congo and Niger rivers on the basis of that established on the Danube and other international rivers; and, third: What formalities should be observed in order to further effective occupations of territory on the African coasts. In connection with the Government of the French Republic invitations were issued to, and accepted by, twelve national governments, which with the inviting powers, constituted a Conference of fourteen nations, in which the minor countries like Denmark and Holland had a voice and veto equal to that of the Great Powers. All questions of forms of government and of territorial right or jurisdiction were excluded from the consideration of the Conference. No dynastic question could be considered. The only non-commercial question before them, if indeed this were not also one, was that which affected the governments intending hereafter to occupy parts of the

African coasts. To them was addressed the inquiry, what will you agree to do to make certain your occupation of any part of the coast? Every government represented was left absolutely free to agree or disagree with the results of the Conference.

The United States very wisely participated in its deliberations for the protection of its own commercial interests, present and future, against colonial exclusiveness and for the promotion of those views which had already induced the President and Senate to recognize the first free government established in Central Africa. The assembled delegates naturally divided themselves into two groups: those whose governments had colonized or intended to colonize that region, and would therefore like to control its trade, like France and Portugal; and those who, like the United States, only wished for their people liberty of access and equal rights of trade, and the free exercise of their religion and civilizing influences in that newly discovered country. The only essential differences arose from this conflict of interests which at one time threatened to be serious. Under the wise guidance of the German delegates and with the aid of discreet and temperate diplomatists like those representing Italy, England, and Belgium, accord was finally established. . . .

The first of the declarations of the Conference relates to the "liberty of commerce in the basin of the Congo, its embouchures and neighboring countries, together with certain dispositions connected therewith."

This declaration constitutes an agreement on the part of all the governments adhering to it that the commerce of each of their nations shall enjoy complete liberty in all the region drained by the Congo and its affluents. . . .

It was also agreed that all flags without distinction of nationality shall have free access to all the shores of the above territories; to all their rivers flowing into the sea; to all the waters of the Congo and its affluents, and to the lakes, and all connecting canals which shall be made and to all the ports on their borders; with liberty of coasting trade and boating by sea and river. No other taxes should be imposed than as an equivalent for the expenses incurred for the benefit of commerce itself. And every sort of differential treatment of ships and merchandise is prohibited. All kinds of commercial monopoly and exceptional privilege are agreed to be forbidden. Absolute equality among nations is established and their commercial rights are to be the same as those of the possessory government. Strangers shall have the same personal rights as the allegiants for pursuing their professions, for acquiring and transmitting property, both personal and real, and generally shall enjoy the same protection and the same treatment.

Not only do the possessory powers agree to all this. They further pledge themselves to care for the preservation of the native races and for the amelioration of their moral and material condition, and to strive for the suppression of slavery, and especially of the slave trade. They pledge themselves to protect and favor, without distinction of nationality or forms of worship, all religions, scientific and charitable enterprises tending to the instruction and civilization of the natives. The possessory powers further guarantee liberty of conscience and religious toleration to natives and strangers and citizens, together with the right of all to erect places of worship and to organize missions without any restriction.

To what of all this does the Secretary of State object? What is there in it that is not profoundly acceptable to the American People? Is it not the very substance of the American Constitution extended to the heart of Africa? . . .

We secure freedom and equality for our vessels and our commerce in all time and through all progressive developments to come, in an area broader than the United States and extending from the Atlantic to the Indian Ocean, together with all its interior waters, and over the canals and railroads connecting them. We secure the abolition of all monopolies, private or corporate. This is to continue, whatever the present sovereign jurisdiction, or the changes of governments to come, and whether they be independent states or colonial dependencies, and in time of war as well as peace. We secure freedom and equal protection for the persons of Americans whether traveling or resident there, for their property, and for the pursuit of their professions and enterprises of every sort. We gain security for the American missionaries, churches, and schools, now or hereafter to be established, and absolute liberty of commerce and freedom of worship. We gain pledges for the extinction of the hateful slave trade. In a word, we gain everything which we could gain by owning the country, except the expense of governing it. What we gain here by adhering to this act is what elsewhere we have been for one hundred years unable to gain by special negotiations with each individual government, from whose colonial possessions we are until this day either excluded or only admitted upon ruinous terms of discrimination.

On the other hand, what do we yield in exchange for this? Neither land, nor soldiers; neither money nor liability to expenditure; neither jurisdiction nor revenue. We simply agree to recognize in other nations the same rights in Central Africa which are conceded to us; and we agree to use our "good offices" with the governments on the eastern coast to obtain their consent to apply the liberal provisions of the act to their territories: in other words, to further our own interests. We further agree to lend our "good offices"—*bons offices,* says the text and only that—to persuade a belligerent having possessions in this free zone, and with the consent of both belligerents, to adopt neutrality for these possessions during any war. These are the engagements, and the only engagements for action, which we assume toward other governments. But this pledge of our "good offices" is hardly startling enough to shock the timidity of an administration which represents the spirit of the American people.

The only grounds upon which the President is made to rest his objections to the work of the Conference *do not exist.* If they existed the work ought not to be and would not be ratified by the Senate. Being non-existent the act should be approved by both President and Senate in justice to the present and future interests of the United States, and in the interest of civilization itself. If too late to adopt it by simple ratification, it should be accepted by a "separate act," for which it makes provision.

(From *The North American Review,* February, 1886, CXLII, 119-133)

HUGH McCULLOCH, "Report of the Secretary of the Treasury," 1884

It was not many years after the first cotton-mills were erected in New England that the great iron interests of the country began to be developed, and Pennsylvania soon became the great iron-manufacturing State of the Union. Nor was it long before various kinds of manufactures came into existence in most of the Northern and Western States. The demands of the Government during the late civil war for nearly all kinds of manufactured goods and the high tariff greatly stimulated production. After the war, stimulus was found in railroad building and in extravagant expenditures induced by superabundant currency, and the time has now come when the manufacturing industry of the United States is in dire distress from a plethora of manufactured goods. Some manufacturing companies have been forced into bankruptcy; others have closed their mills to escape it; few mills are running on full time, and as a consequence a very large number of operatives are either deprived of employment or are working for wages hardly sufficient to enable them to live comfortably or even decently. Nor are manufacturers and their employés the only sufferers by the present depression of our manufacturing industry. So large and widespread has this industry become, so interwoven is it with other industries, so essential is it to the welfare of the whole country, that it cannot be seriously depressed without injuriously affecting business throughout the Union.

The all-important question, therefore, that presses itself upon the public attention is, how shall the country be relieved from the plethora of manufactured goods, and how shall plethora hereafter be prevented? It is obvious that our power to produce is much in excess of the present or any probable future demand for home consumption. The existing iron, cotton, and woollen mills, if employed at their full capacity, could meet in six months—perhaps in a shorter time—the home demand for a year. It is certain, therefore, that unless markets now practically closed against us are opened; unless we can share in the trade which is monopolized by European nations, the depression now so severely felt will continue, and may become more disastrous.

The question how shall our foreign trade be increased is the question which now comes to the front and demands prompt and careful consideration. Manufacturers are primarily interested, but the whole country has a stake in its solution. In its investigation the tariff will necessarily be involved, inasmuch as the relations between it and our foreign trade are so close that they cannot be considered separately, but it need not be involved except so far as it stands in the way of international trade. If the duties upon raw materials are an obstruction, those duties should be removed. If the duties upon other articles are an obstruction, they should be modified. Whatever may be required to increase our foreign trade, whether it be a repeal or modification of existing duties, should be demanded by the manufacturers themselves. How, then, shall the information required for a full understanding of what stands in the way of an increased exportation of our manufactured goods be obtained? It may not be proper for me to offer advice on this point, but I cannot forbear to say that I can see no better means than by the appointment of a Commission, composed of men not wedded to the doctrines of free trade or protection—fair-minded men, who would prosecute the inquiry thoroughly, comprehensibly, and impartially. If such a Commission should be created, it should be done without unnecessary delay. . . .

The business of the whole world has been revolutionized by steam-power and the substitution of machinery for hand-work. If not the inventor of the steam-engine, Great Britain took the lead in utilizing it in manufacturing, and she thus became the great workshop of the world. For many years she had a monopoly of manufacturing. The raw materials from nearly all nations were taken in her own ships to her ports and returned in manufactured goods. It has been the profit of this combination of manufactures and commerce which has made her the richest and most powerful of nations. Now, however, all western nations are endeavoring to use their raw materials at home and to encourage and sustain their manufactures by protective duties, the effect of which has been general overproduction.

It is this great revolution caused by steam-power and machinery and their general use that will make the labors of the Commission so arduous. All the leading nations of the world are now engaged in manufacturing, and all but Great Britain are fencing themselves in by protective duties. Among them the United States has been conspicuous. Has not the time come when a new departure is demanded? Cobden, one of the ablest and most farseeing of British statesmen, predicted that the United States would in time not only become a great manufacturing country, but would become a competitor with Great Britain in the South American markets. In the course of some remarks upon the condition of British trade he said:

Members of the House of Commons and others are constantly crying out that there is very great danger threatening this country from Russia, and they neglect to observe that the great danger to the supremacy of the country is not in Russia, but in the competition of the United States of America.

The Cobden Club is the channel through which the free-trade sentiments of Great Britain find expression, and yet, at a recent meeting of the club, the following language by one of the prominent members of Parliament was cheered and applauded:

> Many persons seem to think that the effect of the reduction of the protective duties in America would be to enable us to flood the United States with our productions. For a short time probably it would give a stimulus to our trade, but in the long run the effect of it would be to cheapen American productions, and to increase the competition of America with us in other parts of the world. We should have to meet that competition. We should find the Americans very serious competitors, and we should have in this country to throw aside many of the bonds which now fetter our industry.

The present condition of our foreign trade is not as fully understood by the public as it ought to be, or there would be greater uneasiness in regard to what may be the result. Look, for instance, at our trade relations with Brazil. We sold to Brazil last year various articles to the amount of $8,645,261. We bought of her various kinds of her own productions to the amount of $50,265,889, leaving $41,620,628 as the balance against us. Now, how is this large balance liquidated? Not by gold, but by the sale of our farm products, for which there is a large demand in Europe. It is our cotton, our wheat, our petroleum, our beef and pork, which can be produced more cheaply in the United States than anywhere else, which create the sterling exchange that enables us to carry on this one-sided trade with Brazil. Now, if by the failure of our crops, or very favorable seasons on the other side of the Atlantic, or, what is more probable, by retaliation, our exports of these articles should materially decline, what then would be the condition of our Brazilian trade? Instead of depending upon the exports to Europe for the means to cover the balance in favor of Brazil, ought not an effort be made to equalize that trade by our manufactured goods? Ought we not to endeavor to verify the prediction of Cobden by becoming a competitor with Great Britain in the Brazilian markets? Ought not this to be attempted in the interest of our own manufacturers?

Reference is made to our trade with Brazil because it is much larger than that with other South American States, but our trade with all of them is of the same one-sided and unsatisfactory character. Ought it so to continue? The South American States are our neighbors. With the exception of Brazil, their institutions are moulded upon ours. They would be glad to establish close trade relations with us, which could not fail to be of mutual advantage; and yet so little intercourse have we with them that supplies for our ships-of-war in South American ports must be paid for in sterling exchange. . . .

In competition with Great Britain in the South American markets, Great Britain will have the advantage by being already in possession of the trade, but this advantage will doubtless be counterbalanced by the abundance and comparative cheapness of our agricultural productions. That we are to be a competitor with Great Britain in foreign markets, especially in the markets of the South American States, is as certain as anything in the future can be. The steps which may be needful to make this competition successful it will be for Congress to determine after the Commission has performed its duty. To me it seems certain that it cannot properly be done before. A nation with fifty-six millions of people, doubling every 25 years, a people distinguished for enterprise and inventive power, in possession of a country of vast extent and rich beyond comparison in developed and undeveloped resources, ought not much longer to be prevented from having a full share in the honor and the gain of international trade.

(From *Report of the Secretary of Treasury, 1884,* Washington, 1885, pp. x-xv)

J. S. JEANS, "The Labour War in the United States," 1894

It has for well on to half a century been one of the greatest boasts of the United States that they possess a self-reliant, a law-abiding, and an industrious people. When the Civil War was over, General Sherman challenged the world to show another case where 1,080,000 men laid down their arms at once and the same time and submitted themselves peaceably to the civil authority. This was, indeed, a circumstance in the history of the nation of which they had just reason to be proud. But the times were exceptionally propitious for such a remarkable manifestation. Industry had been neglected for many years. Agriculture had greatly suffered for lack of willing and competent labour. There was work for all to do, if only they cared to do it. Land was cheap and plentiful, manufacturing industry was ready to absorb an unlimited number of workers, with a system of State protection that stimulated and encouraged enterprise, and the country had achieved a victory over itself that braced up the people to strong, resolute, and sustained endeavour. From this point, indeed, we may date the commencement of that marvellous career of development that the United States have pursued during recent years—a career that has placed the country in the front rank of both agricultural and manufacturing nations, and has made it at once the wonder and the envy of the rest of the world.

Since that memorable period the population of the United States has considerably more than doubled. Its capacity for the production of commodities of every kind has, however, vastly more than doubled. Its agricultural produce has gone out into all the earth. Its manufactures have reached a state of development that causes the oldest countries in Europe to hide their diminished heads. The American people have not only achieved the front rank in agriculture, in mining, in the iron and steel industries, in mechanical industry, in the ownership and administration of railways, and in almost every other adjunct and evidence of material progress, but they have become far and away the richest people that have ever lived at any stage or epoch in the history of the world. In manufacturing industry they had embarked, at the date of the census of 1890, more than 1,305 millions sterling. In railway enterprise they had at the same date expended considerably over 2,000 millions sterling. In agriculture their possessions must be proportionately large, though less readily assessable. They have the largest output of any country on the face of the earth of all the principal minerals, both useful and noble. They have the largest foreign commerce, as measured by exports, except our own country;

and they have a territory so varied in conditions of soil and climate as to be adapted for the growth of almost every commodity that they are likely to require. All this, and the bounding prosperity that has been built upon it during the last thirty years or more, has tended to raise hopes, expectations, and ambitions of the highest kind. The people have known such a long period of prosperity that they are but ill-prepared for the adversity that countries, like individuals, must be equipped and ready to face.

Reverses, like offences, must needs come, however: for more than a generation the United States have had the experience of Dives, and they are scarcely prepared for the more bitter, if not less wholesome, experience of Lazarus. For the last 12 months the vaunted prosperity and stability of the country have appeared to be tumbling down like a house of cards. The prices of commodities, to begin with, have suffered such a fall as has never been known before in the history of any industrial people. Of the extent and the incidence of this collapse we shall have more to say by-and-by. The demand for all descriptions of produce has been seriously curtailed, partly owing to a glut of commodities, partly owing to a serious diminution of the purchasing power of the people. As a consequence, the output of iron, steel, minerals, mechanical products generally, and, indeed, of practically every one of the commodities that had previously appeared to respond to an almost unlimited demand, has seriously fallen off. The output of pig-iron, for example, fell from over nine million to less than six million tons a year. The production of steel has been reduced by nearly one half. The iron-ore mines of Lake Superior have in many cases been entirely closed, and they have been compelled to realise at prices below any that had ever before been known. Agriculture has shared in the general depression; and, as the next largest interest after agriculture, the railways have found it all but impossible to meet their obligations, except in a few special cases, while thousands of miles of line have passed into the hands of receivers.

It was only natural that these unusual phenomena should exercise a malignant and a disturbing influence upon both capital and labour. Of the two, it is not easy to say which has been the most seriously hurt. Capital has disappeared "like a snowflake on the river." Companies and firms whose bonds were up to that time regarded as good for almost any emergency have turned their faces to the wall. The crop of failures has been unprecedentedly large, every interest having more or less suffered. But the function and the habit of capital is to "learn to labour and to wait." When it loses ground, it must patiently plod on until the ground has been recovered again, or, if it is wiped out entirely, it can only submit to the inevitable, and make way for other attempts to "breast the blows of circumstance." With labour, on the contrary, the end and the aim are more immediate. As a rule, labour only seeks to secure an adequate return at the moment, and if that return is not at once forthcoming, it loses patience and often revolts. Such is the condition of things in the United States at the present time. For many months past the areas of remunerative labour have been contracting, in all industries and occupations. In a great majority of cases the rate of wages has been reduced. This, of course, is almost entirely a new experience in a country where wages have been accustomed to advance in harmony with the general conditions of progress. But worse than this remains behind. With the closing of first one mine and then another, with the shutting-down of first one work and then another, throughout every industry and every State, the ranks of the unemployed have been steadily and surely recruited until they formed an army almost, if not quite, as large as that which American history so proudly extols as having returned to peaceful industry after the determining fight had settled the Civil War.

The recent strike of railway *employés* is simply an acute stage and development of a general and deep-seated disorder of the body politic. It has excited more attention than most strikes of the same kind, both because of its more general character, and because of the serious loss and inconvenience that the threatened general disruption of railroad transportation would inevitably entail upon the community as a whole. The agitation extended over many thousands of square miles of territory, and was quite as pronounced and serious in California as in Illinois, or any of the more Eastern States. . . .

Owing to the great influx of emigrant, and generally of more or less pauper, labour into the United States, the country is subject to continual risk of disturbances from which more settled countries are comparatively free. A large proportion of this emigrant population is "agin" all law and order. They owe allegiance to no sovereign and to no country. They have generally had a hard and difficult lot at home, and they have usually left their own land in order that they may establish in the country of their adoption a different order of things. *Coûte que coûte,* they array themselves on the side that appears most likely to promise immediate gain. If unemployed, or enjoying very inadequate earnings, they are not infrequently ready to go to greater extremes in the way of agitation than they would have been with other and more favourable circumstances. The emigrant is in many respects a superior person. The enterprise, the valour, the indifference to the *agréments* of life, and the other qualities of daring and endeavour that have led him to change his home, and seek for a new life in a world of which he generally knows next to nothing, are all liable to abuse under conditions that are every now and again likely to arise in all countries, but are more especially liable to occur under the transitory and kaleidoscopic conditions of life and growth that occur in a country like the United States.

It is manifest, then, that the United States have been, and are, in a special degree likely to remain subject to the constant recrudescence of the labour question. For the United Kingdom this problem has a greater and more enduring interest than appears on the surface. The unceasing and almost unhealthy energy of the American people has already placed them in a position to reconcile their economic system with cheap production in many products that have hitherto been supposed to be almost of purely British growth. American agriculture had displaced English agricultural produce many years ago, and threatens to do so more and more. But the British manufacturer has recently been threatened with the same fate. In the iron, cotton, and other leading industries, American inventiveness, industry, and enterprise have brought American prices almost down to a European level. The cultivation of foreign markets, hitherto disregarded except for agricultural produce, has now become, for American manufacturers, a matter of the most pressing concern. Having filled to overflowing their own previously redundant order-books, they are now adjusting their costs so as to meet Britain in the principal markets of the world. If Britain and the United States are alike sufferers by the restiveness of labour, the competition which we dread may still be some way off, but if Britain were to have a monopoly of labour troubles like the

coal strike of last year, this undesirable and ominous end could not
be long delayed.

(From *Nineteenth Century,* August, 1894, XXXVI, 259-268)

FREDERICK JACKSON TURNER, "The Problem of the West,"
1896

The West, at bottom, is a form of society, rather than an area. It is
the term applied to the region whose social conditions result from
the application of older institutions and ideas to the transforming
influence of free land. By this application, a new environment is
suddenly entered, freedom of opportunity is opened, the cake of custom is broken, and new activities, new lines of growth, new institutions and new ideals, are brought into existence. The wilderness disappears, the "West" proper passes on to a new frontier, and in the
former area, a new society has emerged from its contact with the
backwoods. Gradually this society loses its primitive conditions, and
assimilates itself to the type of the older social conditions of the East:
but it bears within it enduring and distinguishing survivals of its
frontier experience. Decade after decade, West after West, this rebirth
of American society has gone on, has left its traces behind it, and
has reacted on the East. The history of our political institutions, our
democracy, is not a history of imitation, of simply borrowing; it is a
history of the evolution and adaptation of organs in response to
changed environment, a history of the origin of new political species.
In this sense, therefore, the West has been a constructive force of the
highest significance in our life. To use the words of that acute and
widely informed observer, Mr. Bryce, "The West is the most American part of America. . . . What Europe is to Asia, what America
is to England, that the Western States and Territories are to the
Atlantic States. . . .

The separation of the Western man from the seaboard, and his
environment, made him in a large degree free from European
precedents and forces. He looked at things independently and with
small regard or appreciation for the best Old World experience. He

had no ideal of a philosophical, eclectic nation, that should advance civilization by "intercourse with foreigners and familiarity with their point of view, and readiness to adopt whatever is best and most suitable in their ideas, manners, and customs." His was rather the ideal of conserving and developing what was original and valuable in this new country. The entrance of the old society upon free lands meant to him opportunity for a new type of democracy and new popular ideals. The West was not conservative: buoyant self-confidence and self-assertion were distinguishing traits in its composition. It saw in its growth nothing less than a new order of society and state. In this conception were elements of evil and elements of good.

But the fundamental fact in regard to this new society was its relation to land. Professor Boutmy has said of the United States, "Their one primary and predominant object is to cultivate and settle these prairies, forests, and vast waste lands. The striking and peculiar characteristic of American society is that it is not so much a democracy as a huge commercial company for the discovery, cultivation, and capitalization of its enormous territory. The United States are primarily a commercial society, and only secondarily a nation." Of course this involves a serious misapprehension. By the very fact of the task here set forth, far-reaching ideals of the state and of society have been evolved in the West, accompanied by loyalty to the nation representative of these ideals. But M. Boutmy's description hits the substantial fact, that the fundamental traits of the man of the interior were due to the free lands of the West. These turned his attention to the great task of advancing his economic and social status in the new democracy which he was helping to create. Art, literature, refinement, scientific administration, all had to give way to this Titanic labor. Energy, incessant activity, became the lot of this new American. Says a traveler of the time of Andrew Jackson, "America is like a vast workshop, over the door of which is printed in blazing characters, 'No admittance here, except on business.' " The West of our own day reminds Mr. Bryce "of the crowd which Vathek found in the hall of Eblis, each darting hither and thither with swift steps and unquiet mien, driven to and fro by a fire in the heart. Time seems too short for what they have to do, and the result always to come short of their desire."

But free lands and the consciousness of working out their social destiny did more than turn the Westerner to material interests and devote him to a restless existence. They promoted equality among the Western settlers, and reacted as a check on the aristocratic influences of the East. Where everybody could have a farm, almost for taking it, economic equality resulted, and this involved political equality. Not without a struggle would the Western man abandon this ideal, and it goes far to explain the unrest in the remote West to-day. . . .

The Western man believed in the manifest destiny of his country. On his border, and checking his advance, were the Indian, the Spaniard, and the Englishman. He was indignant at Eastern indifference and lack of sympathy with his view of his relations to these peoples; at the short-sightedness of Eastern policy. The closure of the Mississippi by Spain, and the proposal to exchange our claim of freedom of navigating the river, in return for commercial advantages to New England, nearly led to the withdrawal of the West from the Union. It was the Western demands that brought about the purchase of Louisiana, and turned the scale in favor of declaring the War of 1812. Militant qualities were favored by the annual expansion of the settled area in the face of hostile Indians and the stubborn wilderness. The West caught the vision of the nation's continental destiny. Henry Adams, in his *History of the United States,* makes the American of 1800 exclaim to the foreign visitor, "Look at my wealth! See these solid mountains of salt and iron, of lead, copper, silver, and gold. See these magnificent cities scattered broadcast to the Pacific! See my cornfields rustling and waving in the summer breeze from ocean to ocean, so far that the sun itself is not high enough to mark where the distant mountains bound my golden seas. Look at this continent of mine, fairest of created worlds, as she lies turning up to the sun's never failing caress her broad and exuberant breasts, overflowing with milk for her 100 million children." And the foreigner saw only dreary deserts, tenanted by sparse, ague-stricken pioneers and savages. The cities were log huts and gambling dens. But the frontiersman's dream was prophetic. In spite of his rude, gross nature, this early Western man was an idealist withal. He dreamed dreams and beheld visions. He had faith in man, hope for democracy, belief in America's destiny, unbounded confidence in his ability to make his dreams come true. . . .

We are now in a position to see clearly some of the factors involved in the Western problem. For nearly three centuries the dominant fact in American life has been expansion. With the settlement of the Pacific coast and the occupation of the free lands, this movement has come to a check. That these energies of expansion will no longer operate would be a rash prediction; and the demands for a vigorous foreign policy, for an interoceanic canal, for a revival of our power on the seas, and for the extension of American influence to outlying islands and adjoining countries, are indications that the movement will continue. The stronghold of these demands lies west of the Alleghenies.

In the remoter West, the restless, rushing wave of settlement has broken with a shock against the arid plains. The free lands are gone, the continent is crossed, and all this push and energy is turning into channels of agitation. Failures in one area can no longer be made good by taking up land on a new frontier; the conditions of a settled society are being reached with suddenness and with confusion. The West has been built up with borrowed capital, and the question of the stability of gold, as a standard of deferred payments, is eagerly agitated by the debtor West, profoundly dissatisfied with the industrial conditions that confront it, and actuated by frontier directness and rigor in its remedies. For the most part, the men who built up the West beyond the Mississippi, and who are now leading the agitation, came as pioneers from the old Northwest, in the days when it was just passing from the stage of a frontier section. . . . The Western problem is no longer a sectional problem: it is a social problem on a national scale. The greater West, extending from the Alleghenies to the Pacific, cannot be regarded as a unit; it requires analysis into regions and classes. But its area, its population, and its material resources would give force to its assertion that if there is a sectionalism in the country, the sectionalism is Eastern. The old West, united to the new South, would produce, not a new sectionalism, but a new Americanism. It would not mean sectional disunion, as some have speculated, but it might mean a drastic assertion of national government and imperial expansion under a popular hero.

This, then, is the real situation: a people composed of heterogeneous materials, with diverse and conflicting ideals and social interests, having passed from the task of filling up the vacant spaces of the continent, is now thrown back upon itself, and is seeking an equilibrium. The diverse elements are being fused into national unity. The forces of reorganization are turbulent and the nation seems like a witches' kettle.

(From *The Atlantic Monthly*, September, 1896, LXXVIII, 289-297)

WOODROW WILSON, "Make Haste Slowly," Address Delivered April 30, 1889, on the One Hundredth Anniversary of the Inauguration of George Washington

The profitable thing for us to remember is, that, though the saving habit in politics may be acquired by wisdom and sober, steadfast endeavour, which are very rare, it may be lost by folly, which is very common. Evidently wisdom and endeavour have had rare good opportunities in America during the century that is past: wisdom is not difficult where resources are unbounded; endeavour is not arduous where there is exceeding rich reward. But the century which *begins* to-day will doubtless make a very different distribution of its favours among us. It is easier to be new than to be old—far lighter work to be pioneers needing mere muscle and physical courage, than patiently and resolutely to face the problems of a crowded and perplexed civilization. It was easier to drive out an army of English troops than it will be to assimilate a heterogeneous horde of immigrants. It required less self-possession to establish our governments than it will require to maintain them: the principles on which they should be constructed to meet our needs in the beginning were much plainer to see than are the principles upon which they must be modified to meet the needs of the present and future.

For us this is the centennial year of Washington's inauguration; but for Europe it is the centennial year of the French Revolution. One hundred years ago we gained, and Europe lost, self-command, self-possession. But since then we have been steadily receiving into our midst and to full participation in our national life the very people whom their home politics have familiarized with revolution: our own equable blood we have suffered to receive into it the most feverish blood of the restless old world. We are facing an ever-increasing difficulty of self-possession with ever deteriorating materials: for your only reliable stuff in this strain of politics is Character.

(From *The Public Papers of Woodrow Wilson,* New York, 1925, I, 184-185)

WOODROW WILSON, "The Making of the Nation," July, 1897

The conviction is becoming painfully distinct among us, moreover, that these contrasts of condition and differences of interest between the several sections of the country are now more marked and emphasized than they ever were before. The country has been transformed within a generation, not by any creations in a new kind, but by stupendous changes in degree. Every interest has increased its scale and its individual significance. The "East" is transformed by the vast accumulation of wealth made since the civil war,—transformed from a simple to a complex civilization, more like the Old World than like the New. The "West" has so magnified its characteristics by sheer growth, every economic interest which its life represents has become so gigantic in its proportions, that it seems to Eastern men, and to its own people also, more than ever a region apart. It is true that the "West" is not, as a matter of fact, a region at all, but, in Professor Turner's admirable phrase, a stage of development, nowhere set apart and isolated, but spread abroad through all the far interior of the continent. But it is now a stage of development with a difference, as Professor Turner has shown, which makes it practically a new thing in our history. The "West" was once a series of States and settlements beyond which lay free lands not yet occupied, into which the restless and all who could not thrive by mere steady industry, all who had come too late and all who had stayed too long, could pass on, and, it might be, better their fortunes. Now it lies without outlet. The free lands are gone. New communities must make their life sufficient without this easy escape,—must study economy, find their fortunes in what lies at hand, intensify effort, increase capital, build up a future out of details. It is as if they were caught in a fixed order of life and forced into a new competition, and both their self-consciousness and their keenness to observe every point of self-interest are enlarged beyond former example. . . .

It is to this point we have come in the making of the nation. The old sort of growth is at an end,—the growth by mere expansion. We have now to look more closely to internal conditions, and study the means by which a various people is to be bound together in a single interest. Many differences will pass away of themselves. "East" and "West" will come together by a slow approach, as capital accumulates where now it is only borrowed, as industrial development makes its way westward in a new variety, as life gets its final elaboration and detail throughout all the great spaces of the continent, until all the scattered parts of the nation are drawn into real community of interest. . . .

Much may be brought about by a mere knowledge of the situation. It is not simply the existence of facts that governs us, but consciousness and comprehension of the facts. The whole process of statesmanship consists in bringing facts to light, and shaping law to suit, or, if need be, mould them. It is part of our present danger that men of the "East" listen only to their own public men, men of the "West" only to theirs. We speak of the "West" as out of sympathy with the "East"; it would be instructive once and again to reverse the terms, and admit that the "East" neither understands nor sympathizes with the "West,"—and thorough nationalization depends upon mutual understandings and sympathies. There is an unpleasant significance in the fact that the "East" has made no serious attempt to understand the desire for the free coinage of silver in the "West" and the South. If it were once really probed and comprehended, we should know that it is necessary to reform our currency at once, and we should know in what way it is necessary to reform it; we should know that a new protective tariff only marks with a new emphasis the contrast in economic interest between the "East" and the "West," and that nothing but currency reform can touch the cause of the present discontents. . . .

(From *The Public Papers of Woodrow Wilson,* New York, 1925, I, 313-314, 328-329)

NEW YORK BOARD OF TRADE, "Resolution Submitted to the National Board of Trade," December, 1897

RESOLVED: That the National Board of Trade calls attention with pleasure to the gratifying increase in our export trade, especially in manufactured products, which embody not only the use of American raw materials, but the employment of American labor. The quality and utility of American products are recognized wherever they are known. The ingenuity of our inventors has produced thousands of articles of superior economy and convenience, which, if intelligently presented to the 1,370 millions of consumers who exist outside of the United States, would find a market. That the same methods of publicity and personal representation pursued in the introduction of goods in this country will prove effective when applied abroad. That through associated effort much can be accomplished, and hence commend all such efforts; and our Government should lead in the policy of developing foreign markets for our products.

BOSTON MERCHANTS ASSOCIATION, "Resolution," 1897

The Boston Merchants Association, which for many years has taken the leading position in behalf of better commercial relations with Canada, is greatly interested in the mission of Sir Wilfred Laurier, Premier of Canada, and his associates, to our Government in Washington. We have felt that the advent to power of this gentleman, and the liberal party of the Dominion should result in greatly enlarged intercourse with our neighbors, whose common relations to the American continent should make them as truly Americans as ourselves. We are in hearty sympathy with Sir Wilfred's purpose to remove, if possible, *all* matters of difference or controversy between us, and we bespeak for him and his associates the most favorable reception by this administration. We are unalterably convinced that the magnificent resources of the entire North American continent can, by a wise reciprocity between the United States and Canada, be made available for the unity, the prosperity, and the progress of the entire North American people.

NATIONAL BOARD OF TRADE, "Resolution on China," 1900

WHEREAS, Certain of the leading nations of the Old World have given indications of a desire to parcel out the great empire of China for their own special benefit, and within their spheres of influence in that great country prevent commerce with the United States and all other nations but themselves; and

WHEREAS, The Empire of China embraces 400 millions of people, or one-quarter of the human family, and the trade which may be developed with that country cannot fail to be of immense importance;

RESOLVED, That the National Board of Trade expresses its firm conviction that the United States should use all the influence it can in the field of diplomacy to prevent such a cutting up for selfish purposes of the Chinese Empire, and co-operate with those nations which insist on the trade of that great country being open to all the nations of the world on equal terms.

AARON JONES, Master of the National Grange, "Testimony," 1899

. . . We also want a widening of the markets for the farmers. We feel that the great power of this Government and very large sums of money have been expended to widen the market for our manufacturing industries in foreign countries. We believe there should be no discrimination and that the same energies and efforts ought to be put forward by the Government for advancing the markets of agriculture in all foreign countries. Men in the consular service ought to be sent abroad with the view of ascertaining what the market requires in the various countries, the probable demand of this country for importation and the probable supplies it might have for export, so as to advise this country. Farmers are placed at a disadvantage, compared with the commercial interests of the country, because they are slower in learning the demand of the world for the products they have in hand than are the commercial interests. We believe it is within the legitimate province of the Government to protect all its citizens alike, and we believe that no man should be appointed in the consular service who is not imbued with the importance of agricultural products equally with manufactured goods. . . . We believe it is within the province of this Government to see that when any discrimination in any of the laws of foreign countries are made against the interests of the agriculture of the United States, this Government should protect us by proper methods. . . .

(From *Report of the Industrial Commission on Agriculture and Agricultural Labor,* Washington, 1901, X, 32, 38)

The Manufacturers' Record, "Southern Trade in China," October 20, 1899

At two widely-separated points in this country during the past week the importance of the South as a contributor to the foreign trade of the United States and its interest in the further extension of that trade have been clearly shown. Aside from the purely technical papers presented at the Montreal meeting of the New England Cotton Manufacturers' Association, the most important paper was probably that on export trade, read by Mr. D. A. Tompkins of Charlotte, N. C. He alluded to the difficulties under which this country had built up trade with the Far East, expressed the belief that the most vital questions concerning the cotton-mill industry of this country lie along the lines of the republic's making sure of its export trade, and said that no section of the republic was more interested in the policy of the retention of Cuba, Porto Rico and the Philippines than the Southern States. Sustaining the contention which Mr. Tompkins has made for some months is a remarkable and most significant correspondence between cotton-mill men of South Carolina urging the senators and representatives of that State in Congress to do all in their power that the United States may enjoy the "open-door" policy in China. The signers of the letter were John B. Cleveland of the Whitney Manufacturing Co.; John H. Montgomery, president and treasurer of the Pacolet Manufacturing Co. and Spartan Mill; H. D. Wheat, president and treasurer of the Gaffney Manufacturing Co.; J. A. Carroll, president of the Cherokee Falls Manufacturing Co.; R. R. Brown, president and treasurer of the Cowpens Manufacturing Co.; George F. Coffin, president and treasurer of the Enoree Manufacturing Co.; W. E. Lucas, president and treasurer of the Laurens Cotton Mills. Impressed with the importance of the textile industry in South Carolina, these representatives of the industry in the South wrote:

"The business of cotton manufacturing is the paramount manufacturing interest of the State. Next to agriculture it is the principal employment of our people. It returns wages directly to a very large percentage of our population, and indirectly it is the support of many thousands more. A large number of the mills in this State are making goods for the China or Eastern trade. If by any chance this demand should be cut off, the mills would be compelled to shut down, or to get into direct competition with the other mills which are making goods for home consumption. You can see at once what the importance of the China trade is to us; it is everything. The prosperity of the cotton-mill business of South Carolina depends, in our opinion, upon the China trade. We believe that the expansion of this trade is the hope of the cotton-mill industry in the South.

"According to the best of our information, the question of the continuance of this trade is a question of policy on the part of our government. Statistics show that 90 per cent of all the cotton goods exported from the United States to China find a distributing market at the three northern treaty ports of Newchwang, Chefoo and Tientsin. The first named is the treaty port of the great province of Manchuria, already recognized in the railroad and mining enterprises as an exclusive sphere of Russian enterprise. The second is the treaty port of the province of Shantung, in which Germany claims exclusive privileges similar to those conceded to Russia in Manchuria. The third is the treaty port of the metropolitan province of Chili, and is the maritime gate of Peking. All three are situated within a comparatively narrow area, but through them is done most of the foreign trade of North

China. It only requires one step forward in the extension of the authority of Russia and Germany to destroy the terms of equality on which the commercial nations of the world participate in the advantages of Newchwang and Chefoo, and the movement on Peking, which is generally assumed to be part of the policy of Russia, would necessarily threaten the commercial interests which center at Tientsin.

"Up to this time we are informed that pressure brought by the governments of Great Britain and the United States has led Russia to declare its purpose to admit the merchandise of other nations into Manchuria on terms of equality with its own, but it is impossible to say how soon that policy may be changed. It is alleged that in the importation of railroad and other material Russia entirely disregards the imperial Chinese customs of Newchwang, regarding the port as if it were already in a Russian possession; and it may be that Russia, for the protection of its own trade, may see fit to carry this discrimination to the point of imposing her own custom duties on American cotton goods. In such an event our trade with Manchuria would be seriously handicapped, and might, conceivably, cease to exist, as did our trade under like circumstances with Madagascar.

"The effect of this would be a far-reaching one to the cotton-mill industry in the South. Up to this time the federal government has shown a disposition to insist on the maintenance of its treaty rights with the Chinese empire whenever there seemed any danger of their positive infringement, but as we have indicated, the process of substituting for the authority of the Chinese government the jurisdiction of a foreign power is a gradual and insidious one, and its completion would mark the disappearance of all pre-existing treaties."

They contended that the question of maintaining our treaty rights in China was not one of empire, but simply of trade and of the right that Americans now enjoy to conduct a profitable commerce with the Chinese empire. In reply to this letter Senator McLaurin, agreeing fully with its contention, wrote as follows:

"The 'open-door policy' is what we need and want. This has heretofore been secured by 'treaty rights,' which have been respected by other nations only to the extent to which it conduced to their trade interest. While ostensibly recognizing these 'treaty rights,' other nations, in violation of them, have acquired territory and excluded therefrom our legitimate commerce. Russia has gradually absorbed Manchuria and is building a railroad across Siberia to command the trade of China. Germany has been active and waiting in expectancy to obtain the Philippines. Japan has given Russia all the fruits of her victory of 1895. France has been the willing tool of Russia, and England has been passive in her fear to assail her.

"This was the status in the East when the battle of Manila occurred. This victory thwarted all the schemes of Russia for the dismemberment of China, and rendered its absorption and partition impossible. If you want the 'open door,' the United States now holds the key. The archipelago of the Philippines lies along the coast of Asia for 800 miles, and commands it. Manila is the point in the East which is the center of ocean traffic. It is the only point where foreign nations could have obtained commercial stations without a struggle.

"In the vicissitudes and good fortune of a war with Spain, and without any intention of doing so, the United States has acquired the possession of the Philippines, which gives to her paramount political and commercial advantages.

"My judgment is that the control of them, or at least of some portions, is the only safeguard for our trade interests in the East. The abandonment of them means the dismemberment of China, its partition among the European powers, and the inevitable loss of our Chinese trade. . . .

"I do not favor the adoption by this country of a colonial policy, because of the vexed and threatening problems growing out of it, but I do think that, if possible, the United States should maintain sufficient interests in the islands to command equal trade rights with other nations in China. This will prevent for a long time the dismemberment of this vast empire. England and Japan favor the integrity of the empire, but they alone cannot guarantee it against the other European powers. With the weight of the influence of the United States thrown against dismemberment, it would be rendered impossible.

"At present Hong Kong, under British influence, is the great distributing center of the Orient. Manila, under American influence, will occupy a better strategic and geographic position, and should become a commercial center of that portion of the world. Commercial supremacy is the goal of every civilized nation; it is only attained through commercial progress and commercial expansion. In this great battle among the nations, without design of our own, while they were haggling among themselves, Dewey sails into Manila bay, and we find foothold within two days' journey of this land of consumers, where half of the population of the world is congregated within an area no larger than the United States.

"There is much political rot in the constant parading of the term 'imperialism.' It is a misnomer, intended to confuse and deceive. It involves the idea of the incorporation into our body politic as American citizens millions of the semi-barbarous inhabitants of a tropical country. I do not believe such a thing is intended, possible or desirable; nor is such a result necessary to secure such commercial expansion as we want. I think the dictates of common sense will govern the American people, and the ghost 'imperialism,' sprung for political effect, will not prevent them from gathering the full fruits of the victory so easily won, and treading the path so plainly blazed out by an overruling Providence.

"I am willing to concede honesty of purpose and sincerity of conviction to others on these questions. It is difficult for a representative to view this question as he should while the war is in progress, and both parties attempting to make political capital out of it—one making frantic appeals to 'stand by the flag' and the other criticising on humanitarian grounds everything that is said or done. When these questions are considered by Congress it is my purpose to act and vote for what I conceive to be for the best interests of South Carolina. A discharge of duty to the best of my ability will come up to the full measure of my obligations. . . .

"It will be observed, therefore, that the question of our trade in the East involves both political and commercial consequences. Upon its settlement, in my judgment, depends the future welfare of our people in maintaining equality of opportunity in the Eastern markets. A mere superficial view will not reveal its transcendent importance. To the Southern people it is fraught with momentous consequences. Cotton manufacturing in the South has grown in a few years with phenomenal rapidity. Millions of dollars are now invested in mills.

"The product of these have found remunerative markets in China and other countries of the East, our cotton goods being peculiarly adapted for clothing the teeming millions of that warm climate. Their trade is the hope of this great manufacturing industry of the South. If it is cut off by other nations, not only the manufacturer, but the producer of raw cotton will suffer."

This correspondence not only illustrates the view regarding the importance to this country of China trade held by conservative but progressive men of the South, but is a powerful argument from a most practical standpoint against the agitation of those persons who for political reasons, from a spirit of mere opposition or because of actual scruples based upon lack of information, are endeavoring to prevent the United States from enjoying the perfectly legitimate fruits of Dewey's victory in Manila bay.

II

The Debate on
Ways and Means

To PICK up the threads of this debate it is necessary to go back to Grover Cleveland's Annual Message for 1896, which cut through the swelling emotional build-up to the hard question then before the American nation: What should the President and Congress do if the revolution in Cuba was not soon brought to an end? Continuation of that bitter struggle between Spain and its angered subjects, warned the President, threatened to engulf the whole island in its destructive flames. But before the United States would allow Cuba to become its own funeral pyre, he concluded, it would answer a higher call from that unhappy island than its normal obligation to Spanish sovereignty could command. The fires did not subside by the time William Mc-Kinley assumed the presidency, nor did he alter the definition his predecessor had issued outlining the only course open to the United States.

From the tone of the 1896 Message it appeared quite evident that President Cleveland could not bring himself to believe that Madrid's attempts to pacify Cuba would succeed; he offered American good offices, probably on the assumption that he was actually providing Spain an honorable and (under the circumstances) a graceful way out of its too demanding responsibilities in the Western Hemisphere. This renewed civil war in the Caribbean had indeed convinced a great many American leaders that Spain's rule in the new world was no longer effective—and therefore no longer tolerable. From the earliest days of independent nationhood United States policy-makers had determined to oppose and block any attempt to transfer Cuba to some other, more powerful, European nation. Spain's presence there could be allowed only so long as it did not threaten American policy, present or future.

American property interests in Cuba, as Cleveland pointedly remarked, were now second only to those of Spain itself. An article in the *Prairie Farmer* only days before the outbreak of the Spanish-American War detailed these interests from the farmer's point of view.

American sympathies were against Madrid's harsh, repressive measures against the islanders, and Americans were thus involved in the struggle and its outcome. And, most important of all, Americans were more than ever before defining their own well-being and prosperity in terms of peace and stability not in the United States alone, but in the whole of the Americas and the Caribbean Ocean. This Administration had already served notice to the British Empire to that effect over the Venezuelan boundary dispute; even earlier it had moved its naval power into Brazilian ports in order to influence a revolutionary situation toward its own interests against those of European powers.

An outstanding feature of the Cuban crisis, of course, was that American leaders now viewed Caribbean policy in relation to the growing certainty that an Isthmian Canal would soon be attempted. And in so doing they came to the conclusion that Cuban rule over Cuba might not be effective either—especially if left to the temptations of European rivals. The same was true concerning the other large island of the Caribbean, Hispaniola (Santo Domingo and Haiti), and pressures were building to demand a stronger grip there as well In a few years the United States had a naval base in Cuba and was seeking one in Santo Domingo; it had fiscal control over Cuba through the Platt Amendment and over Santo Domingo through the Roosevelt customs arrangement; economic control through trade and investments completed this first phase of the conversion of the Caribbean to an American lake.

One of the policy-makers of these and later years, John Bassett Moore, wrote an incisive review of the unfolding events leading up to the Spanish-American War; it is not only a good debunking account of that series of occurrences and the forces underlying them, but also opens windows onto the broader discussions which took shape in the midst of the sound and the fury over Cuba. Moving from the narrowest issue resulting from the war itself—was America prepared

to accept colonial responsibilities in Cuba, and in the Far East as well?
—these leaders came to an even more fateful crossroads: What direction should American expansion take, given an acceptance of the
proposition that some political control in Cuba and the Philippines
was a necessary adjunct to any policy? Some argued that it would best
find its way in the world through political alliances, but others insisted
that colonial (or naval base–coaling station) expansion alone would
permit the United States to retain freedom of action indefinitely.
Charles Beard once called this approach "Imperial Isolation." In the
end, a consensus developed around the open-door policy, but the
debate within that agreement continued even after 1900.

On one side of the debate were those who opposed any territorial
additions outside the North American continent, but whose views
nonetheless made a contribution to the open-door policy. Among them
was the social Darwinist thinker, William Graham Sumner, whose
well known *laissez-faire* ideas carried over into foreign policy. Professor Sumner always contended that his imperialist opponents failed
to see the differences "between the economic use and the political
jurisdiction" of undeveloped areas, largely because they were being
consumed by an unreasoning "Earth Hunger." To the contrary, asserted
Sumner, the very best thing for Americans would be if the British
extended their rule over all the remaining areas of the world—even
including Cuba. When that was accomplished, Americans could peacefully enjoy all the benefits of expansion, but escape all the political
liabilities of imperialism. Great Britain had had long experience governing such areas; the United States, with its constitutional limitations,
was simply not properly suited to such a role. He further clarified these
opinions in "The Fallacy of Territorial Extension." Americans should
not have troubled themselves over the situation in Cuba, if they could
have been assured of safe access to the island just as they had in
Louisiana where peace and order obtained: "What private individuals
want is free access, under order and security, to any part of the earth's
surface, in order that they may avail themselves of its natural resources
for their use, either by investment or commerce."

Of course the primary gap in Sumner's logic occurred at the outset,
in his very premise. In a world moved by the desires of self-interested
industrial nations, how could an individual expect to secure such

entry, unless backed up directly by gunboats or indirectly through an imposed colonial regime? In theory international *laissez-faire* had a striking appeal; in practice it assumed an equality or par among nations which had never existed. The already intense nationalisms of the nineteenth century, further stimulated by the search for new dominion overseas, made Sumner's model for international behavior an extremely utopian one.

What Sumner was getting at later became the open-door policy, but Alabama's Senator John T. Morgan, though opposed to Philippine annexation, knew that the United States had to have a naval base there to make such a plan work. He called this policy "Freedom of the Seas," a particularly interesting definition of a principle Woodrow Wilson later championed.

Their fellow anti-colonialist, former Secretary of State Richard Olney, also supported Sumner's belief that the pressing need was not land but an extension of the marketplace. Beyond that agreement, however, Olney launched an attack against those who supported the "Imperial Isolationist" position. Their short-sighted reluctance to break with the dogmas built up around the Farewell Address and the Monroe Doctrine alarmed him.

Reviewing the fate of the proposed Congo Convention, Olney warned that the United States could not continue shrugging off obligations under the protection of those documents. Political isolation and freedom of commerce were compatible in the early history of the nation, a time when the individual's ability to fend for himself in the world at large was at a high point. But in the coming century such a combination was not possible. A nation must either opt for total self-containment, political *and* commercial, or it must step forth ready to join the leading powers in the tasks of making the accepted order function smoothly and bringing about needed changes when it did not. Like others, Olney also believed that the United States might participate in world affairs in conjunction with the British Empire, but not if it wanted to use that Empire for unpleasant duties in places like Cuba, a not totally unwarranted extension of Sumner's position.

Fresh from service on McKinley's Peace Commission, Whitelaw Reid defended the annexation of the Philippine Islands as an affirmation of, not a departure from, past policies: "The door is wide open now, and has been ever since Livingston in Paris jumped at Talleyrand's offer to sell him the wilderness west of the Mississippi instead of the settlement eastward to Florida. . . ."

"Yes, but wide open to what?" Olney would no doubt have returned sharply. This was the very point the former Secretary of State had been grappling with. "Wide open to the creation of an Asiatic Empire?" If so, then it was a mistaken policy based upon false assumptions. America was already an empire unto itself. The real goal was to secure the trade of China and an Asiatic Empire would hinder its achievement. For one thing, the United States could more consistently demand equality of opportunity in China if it had no exclusive rights of its own in the Philippines. These islands simply could not support an Asian policy which would satisfy the needs of the United States. In the final accounting, it would be seen that the way to the riches of Asia was through co-operation with the British Empire.

William Jennings Bryan's delimitation of the main campaign issue in the *North American Review* during the summer of 1900 brought strong moral pressure to bear upon the colonialists and no doubt expressed the opinions held by a great many Americans, but his presentation was less clear-cut than was at first thought by historians. Olney, for example, had wanted it clearly understood that an attempt to maintain American possession of the islands in any way was also an effort to sustain, paradoxically, the isolationist mythology of the Farewell Address and the Monroe Doctrine. Bryan, on the other hand, while roundly denouncing the war against Philippine nationalists, clouded the basic issue by suggesting a Monroe Doctrine for the islands until they could stand alone in the world!

Theodore Roosevelt, among others, quickly picked up Bryan's argument and threw it back at the anti-colonialists with the charge that such a plan would be the worst of all the possible choices Washington could make: To begin with it would encourage other powers to venture intrusions to test out the American commitment to an Asian "Monroe Doctrine." Every time that happened the United States would risk losing the islands or face the equally discouraging prospect of armed conflict. As Roosevelt well knew, that kind of dilemma in Cuba and in all of Latin America was challenging enough for any President without adding Asian troubles to his burdens.

And even Olney reluctantly admitted that "The thing is done," and prepared to live with the idea that most American leaders felt the Philippines were an important part of their Asian policy as enunciated by Secretary of State Hay in 1899 and 1900. Most of Hay's advisers did not assume with Whitelaw Reid that the islands were so important in themselves; they preferred to base their policy upon the open-door notes, leaving the questions of alliances or independent action to be worked out. Similarly, it would be necessary to discuss tariff reciprocity, ship subsidies, and finally a Great White Fleet.

GROVER CLEVELAND, "Annual Message," 1896

The insurrection in Cuba still continues with all its perplexities. It is difficult to perceive that any progress has thus far been made toward the pacification of the island or that the situation of affairs as depicted in my last annual message has in the least improved. If Spain still holds Havana and the seaports and all the considerable towns, the insurgents still roam at will over at least two-thirds of the inland country. If the determination of Spain to put down the insurrection seems but to strengthen with the lapse of time and is evinced by her unhesitating devotion of largely increased military and naval forces to the task, there is much reason to believe that the insurgents have gained in point of numbers and character and resources and are none the less inflexible in their resolve not to succumb without practically securing the great objects for which they took up arms. If Spain has not yet reestablished her authority, neither have the insurgents yet made good their title to be regarded as an independent state. Indeed, as the contest has gone on the pretense that civil government exists on the island, except so far as Spain is able to maintain it, has been practically abandoned. Spain does keep on foot such a government, more or less imperfectly, in the large towns and their immediate suburbs; but that exception being made, the entire country is either given over to anarchy or is subject to the military occupation of one or the other party. It is reported, indeed, on reliable authority that at the demand of the commander-in-chief of the insurgent army the putative Cuban government has now given up all attempt to exercise its functions, leaving that government confessedly (what there is the best reason for supposing it always to have been in fact) a government merely on paper.

Were the Spanish armies able to meet their antagonists in the open or in pitched battle, prompt and decisive results might be looked for, and the immense superiority of the Spanish forces in numbers, discipline, and equipment could hardly fail to tell greatly to their advantage. But they are called upon to face a foe that shuns general engagements, that can choose and does choose its own ground, that from the nature of the country is visible or invisible at pleasure, and that fights only from ambuscade and when all the advantages of position and numbers are on its side. In a country where all that is indispensable to life in the way of food, clothing, and shelter is so easily obtainable, especially by those born and bred on the soil, it is obvious that there is hardly a limit to the time during which hostilities of this sort may be prolonged. Meanwhile, as in all cases of protracted civil strife, the passions of the combatants grow more and more inflamed and excesses on both sides become more frequent and deplorable. They are also participated in by bands of marauders, who, now in the name of one party and now in the name of the other, as may best suit the occasion, harry the country at will and plunder its wretched inhabitants for their own advantage. Such a condition of things would inevitably entail immense destruction of property, even if it were the policy of both parties to prevent it as far as practicable; but while such seemed to be the original policy of the Spanish Government, it has now apparently abandoned it and is acting upon the same theory as the insurgents, namely, that the exigencies of the contest require the wholesale annihilation of property that it may not prove of use and advantage to the enemy.

It is to the same end that, in pursuance of general orders, Spanish garrisons are now being withdrawn from plantations and the rural population required to concentrate itself in the towns. The sure result would seem to be that the industrial value of the island is fast diminishing and that unless there is a speedy and radical change in existing conditions it will soon disappear altogether. That value consists very largely, of course, in its capacity to produce sugar—a capacity already much reduced by the interruptions to tillage which have taken place during the last two years. It is reliably asserted that should these interruptions continue during the current year, and practically extend, as is now threatened, to the entire sugar-producing territory of the island, so much time and so much money will be required to restore the land to its normal productiveness that it is extremely doubtful if capital can be induced even to make the attempt.

The spectacle of the utter ruin of an adjoining country, by nature one of the most fertile and charming on the globe, would engage the serious attention of the Government and people of the United States in any circumstances. In point of fact, they have a concern with it which is by no means of a wholly sentimental or philanthropic character. It lies so near to us as to be hardly separated from our territory. Our actual pecuniary interest in it is second only to that of the people and Government of Spain. It is reasonably estimated that at least from $30,000,000 to $50,000,000 of American capital are invested in plantations and in railroad, mining, and other business enterprises on the island. The volume of trade between the United States and Cuba, which in 1889 amounted to about $64,000,000, rose in 1893 to about $103,-000,000, and in 1894, the year before the present insurrection broke out, amounted to nearly $96,000,000. Besides this large pecuniary stake in the fortunes of Cuba, the United States finds itself inextricably involved in the present contest in other ways, both vexatious and costly.

Many Cubans reside in this country, and indirectly promote the insurrection through the press, by public meetings, by the purchase and shipment of arms, by the raising of funds, and by other means which the spirit of our institutions and the tenor of our laws do not permit to be made the subject of criminal prosecutions. Some of them, though Cubans at heart and in all their feelings and interests, have taken out papers as naturalized citizens of the United States—a proceeding resorted to with a view to possible protection by this Government, and not unnaturally regarded with much indignation by the country of their origin. The insurgents are undoubtedly encouraged and supported by the widespread sympathy the people of this country always and instinctively feel for every struggle for better and freer government, and which, in the case of the more adventurous and restless elements of our population, leads in only too many instances to active and personal participation in the contest. The result is that this Government is constantly called upon to protect American citizens, to claim damages for injuries to persons and property, now estimated at many millions of dollars, and to ask explanations and apologies for the acts of Spanish officials whose zeal for the repression of rebellion sometimes blinds them to the immunities belonging to the unoffending citizens of a friendly power. It follows from the same causes that the United States is compelled to actively police a long line of seacoast against unlawful expeditions, the escape of which the utmost vigilance will not always suffice to prevent.

These inevitable entanglements of the United States with the rebellion in Cuba, the large American property interests affected, and considerations of philanthropy and humanity in general have led to a vehement demand in various quarters for some sort of positive intervention on the part of the United States. It was at first proposed that belligerent rights should be accorded to the insurgents—a proposition no longer urged because untimely and in practical operation clearly perilous and injurious to our own interests. It has since been and is now sometimes contended that the independence of the insurgents should be recognized; but imperfect and restricted as the Spanish government of the island may be, no other exists there, unless the will of the military officer in temporary command of a particular district can be dignified as a species of government. It is now also suggested that the United States should buy the island—a suggestion possibly worthy of consideration if there were any evidence of a desire or willingness on the part of Spain to entertain such a proposal. It is urged finally that, all other methods failing, the existing internecine strife in Cuba should be terminated by our intervention, even at the cost of a war between the United States and Spain—a war which its advocates confidently prophesy could neither be large in its proportions nor doubtful in its issue. . . .

It would seem that if Spain should offer to Cuba genuine autonomy —a measure of home rule which, while preserving the sovereignty of Spain, would satisfy all rational requirements of her Spanish subjects— there should be no just reason why the pacification of the island might not be effected on that basis. Such a result would appear to be in the true interest of all concerned. It would at once stop the conflict which is now consuming the resources of the island and making it worthless for whichever party may ultimately prevail. It would keep intact the possessions of Spain without touching her honor, which will be consulted rather than impugned by the adequate redress of admitted grievances. It would put the prosperity of the island and the fortunes of its inhabitants within their own control without severing the natural and ancient ties which bind them to the mother country, and would yet enable them to test their capacity for self-government under the most favorable conditions. It has been objected on the one side that Spain should not promise autonomy until her insurgent subjects lay down their arms; on the other side, that promised autonomy, however liberal, is insufficient, because without assurance of the promise being fulfilled. . . .

Nevertheless, realizing that suspicions and precautions on the part of the weaker of two combatants are always natural and not always unjustifiable, being sincerely desirous in the interest of both as well as on its own account that the Cuban problem should be solved with the least possible delay, it was intimated by this Government to the Government of Spain some months ago that if a satisfactory measure of home rule were tendered the Cuban insurgents and would be accepted by them upon a guaranty of its execution the United States would endeavor to find a way not objectionable to Spain of furnishing such guaranty. While no definite response to this intimation has yet been received from the Spanish Government, it is believed to be not altogether unwelcome, while, as already suggested, no reason is perceived why it should not be approved by the insurgents. Neither party can fail to see the importance of early action, and both must realize that to prolong the present state of things for even a short period will add enormously to the time and labor and expenditure necessary to bring about the industrial recuperation of the island. It is therefore fervently hoped on all grounds that earnest efforts for healing the breach between Spain and the insurgent Cubans upon the lines above indicated may be at once inaugurated and pushed to an immediate and successful issue. The friendly offices of the United States, either in the manner above outlined or in any other way consistent with our Constitution and laws, will always be at the disposal of either party.

Whatever circumstances may arise, our policy and our interests would constrain us to object to the acquisition of the island or an interference with its control by any other power.

It should be added that it can not be reasonably assumed that the hitherto expectant attitude of the United States will be indefinitely maintained. While we are anxious to accord all due respect to the sovereignty of Spain, we can not view the pending conflict in all its features and properly apprehend our inevitably close relations to it and its possible results without considering that by the course of events we may be drawn into such an unusual and unprecedented condition as will fix a limit to our patient waiting for Spain to end the contest, either alone and in her own way or with our friendly cooperation.

When the inability of Spain to deal successfully with the insurrection has become manifest and it is demonstrated that her sovereignty is extinct in Cuba for all purposes of its rightful existence, and when a hopeless struggle for its reestablishment has degenerated into a strife which means nothing more than the useless sacrifice of human life and the utter destruction of the very subject-matter of the conflict, a situation will be presented in which our obligations to the sovereignty of Spain will be superseded by higher obligations, which we can hardly hesitate to recognize and discharge. Deferring the choice of ways and methods until the time for action arrives, we should make them depend upon the precise conditions then existing; and they should not be determined upon without giving careful heed to every consideration involving our honor and interest or the international duty we owe Spain. Until we face the contingencies suggested or the situation is by other incidents imperatively changed we should continue in the line of conduct heretofore pursued, thus in all circumstances exhibiting our obedience to the requirements of public law and our regard for the duty enjoined upon us by the position we occupy in the family of nations.

(From James D. Richardson, *The Messages and Papers of the Presidents,* Washington, 1898, IX, 714-745)

E. S. JONES, "Our Interest in Cuba," 1898

Notwithstanding all that has been said and written about Cuba during the last two years, it is doubtful if a majority of people understand in what the real importance of the island to the United States consists. This, stripped of all questions of sentimentalism, is its trade, with its possible usefulness to us in case of a foreign war. And this trade, it should be said in passing, is of especial importance to the farmers of this country. With normal conditions prevailing, Cuba has been a large consumer of our agricultural products, and should be a much larger consumer of them than heretofore, with the establishment of peace and good government. This will be the more evident when it is remembered that Cuba is within 100 miles of the Florida coast and is easily accessible for the transportation of the many products with which we can supply her 1,800,000 inhabitants, while the mode of transportation is the cheapest of any, namely, water. Flour can be shipped to Cuba from the mills at Minneapolis by the Mississippi river and the Gulf of Mexico, and she is readily accessible from all our Atlantic and gulf ports. In 1893 and 1894 Cuba was a considerable purchaser of American corn, flour, hams, bacon, lard, cars [sic], carriages, steam engines, agricultural implements, builders' hardware, miscellaneous machinery and manufactures of wood. In the fiscal year 1893 her purchases of flour were $2,821,557; hams, $761,082; and lard, $4,023,917, her purchases of these three products of the farm aggregating $7,606,556. Our aggregate exports to Cuba in 1893 were $24,157,698 and in 1894 $20,125,321. While the most of these exports, as the figures indicate, were of goods other than agricultural, in an indirect way even these were of benefit to agriculture, since their production and transportation employed many laborers, skilled and unskilled, a part of whose earnings were necessarily spent in purchases of the products of the farm. On account of the combined influence of the cessation of reciprocity arrangements and the breaking out of the insurrection in the island, our exports to Cuba have fallen off in a marked degree, so that in 1895 they were but $12,533,260, and in 1896 but $7,530,880. . . . This incomplete recital serves to show the promising nature of close commercial relations with Cuba, almost within sight of our shores. It is a market provided by nature for disposing of a part of our surplus agricultural products in exchange for her commodities, some of which we do not produce at all, and others only in inconsiderable quantities. The trade would be in almost every respect mutual, the products of one country conflicting but slightly with those of the other, and so far as the United States are concerned the larger market thus made for our products would amply compensate us for any small competition that might result. . . . The present obstacles to a large and profitable trade with Cuba lie in the disordered state of the island and the heavy duties laid by the Spanish government on imports. If this government could see its way clear to bring peace to the island, it would doubtless be of lasting benefit to both countries, especially if it should succeed in gaining reforms for the Cubans which would relieve them of the onerous exactions of the Spanish government and secure some modification of the tariff imposed on our agricultural products. With peace restored to Cuba, commercial arrangements might be entered into by which our agricultural products should be allowed to enter the island free, or at a low rate of duty, in return for allowing some of her principal products to enter our ports on like terms. In view of the vast underdeveloped wealth of Cuba, some such arrangement could not but be of enduring benefit to the two countries. With the restoration of peace and the establishment of a stable government, capital and labor may reasonably be expected to enter Cuba to develop her resources, with the result of creating large and permanent demand for our agricultural and other products.

(From *The P irie Farmer,* April 2, 1898, p. 2)

JOHN BASSETT MOORE, "Non-Intervention and the Monroe Doctrine," 1904

It may be said that the most pronounced exception ever made by the United States, apart from cases arising under the Monroe Doctrine, to its policy of non-intervention is that which was made in the case of Cuba. At various times since the United States became an independent nation conditions in Cuba had been such as to invite interference either for the purpose of correcting disorders which existed there, or for the purpose of preventing Cuba from falling a prey to some of Spain's European enemies. During the Ten Years' War in Cuba, from 1868 till 1878, intervention by the United States was prevented on several occasions only by the powerful influence of Presi-

dent Grant, counselled and supported by his Secretary of State, Hamilton Fish. In its abstention the administration was aided by the situation
at home, which afforded daily admonition of the difficulties that might
attend the reestablishment of order in a large and populous island
where the process of emancipation was still going on. In 1895 the
situation was changed in the United States as well as in Cuba. American interests on the island had also increased. The second insurrection
was, besides, more active than the first, and spread over a wider area.
If the conflict were left to take its course, the ruin of the island was
apparently assured. The United States tendered its good offices; but the
offer was not productive of any tangible result. In his annual message
of December 7, 1896, President Cleveland declared that, when Spain's
inability to suppress the insurrection had become manifest, and the
struggle had degenerated into a hopeless strife involving useless sacrifice of life and the destruction of the very subject matter of the
conflict, a situation would be presented in which the obligation to
recognize the sovereignty of Spain would be "superseded by higher
obligations."

Conditions continued to grow worse. The distress produced by the
measures of concentration, under the rule of General Weyler, excited
strong feeling in the United States, and prompted President McKinley
to request Spain to put an end to existing conditions and restore order.
General Weyler was afterwards succeeded by General Blanco, and it
was announced that an autonomous regime would be instituted. But
neither the offer of autonomy nor the actual institution of an autonomous government produced peace. The insurgents, embittered by the
three years' conflict, rejected the programme of autonomy with substantial unanimity, while the distinctively Spanish element of the
population viewed it with disapprobation and withdrew from politics.

In this delicate situation the intervention of the United States was
precipitated by certain startling events. The incident created by the
surreptitious publication of the letter of Señor Dupuy de Lome,
Spanish minister at Washington, to Señor Canalejas, in which President
McKinley was aspersed and the reciprocity negotiations between the
two countries were exhibited as a sham, had just been officially declared
to be closed, when the *U.S.S. Maine* was blown up at Havana, and
266 of her crew perished. Shallow and short-sighted reasoners have

wished to treat the destruction of the *Maine* as the justification and the cause of the intervention of the United States. The government of the United States, however, did not itself take that ground. It is true that the case of the *Maine* is mentioned in the preamble to the joint resolution of Congress, by which the intervention of the United States was authorized; but it is recited merely as the culmination of "abhorrent conditions," which had existed for more than three years. The destruction of the *Maine* doubtless kindled the intense popular feeling without which wars are seldom entered upon; but the government of the United States never charged—on the contrary it refrained from charging—that the catastrophe was to be attributed to "the direct act of a Spanish official." Its intervention rested upon the ground that there existed in Cuba conditions so injurious to the United States, as a neighboring nation, that they could no longer be endured. Its action was analogous to what is known in private law as the abatement of a nuisance.

(From *Harper's Magazine,* November, 1904, CIX, 857-869)

WILLIAM GRAHAM SUMNER, "Earth Hunger or the Philosophy of Land Grabbing," 1896

The most important limiting condition on the status of human societies is the ratio of the number of their members to the amount of land at their disposal. It is this ratio of population to land which determines what are the possibilities of human development or the limits of what man can attain in civilization and comfort. . . .

These facts of the social order are of the most fundamental and far-reaching importance. They are the facts which control the fate of the human race and produce the great phenomena which mark ages of history. They are the facts which, since the great geographical explorations of the fifteenth and sixteenth centuries, have spread the population of the European nations over the globe. The most enterprising nations seized the advantage first and have pushed it the farthest. The movements of population have been accelerated by all the inventions which have facilitated transportation and communication. . . .

Earth hunger is the wildest craving of modern nations. They will shed their life blood to appease it. It gratifies national vanity and economic expansion both at once. No reasoning can arrest it, and no arguments satisfy it. At the present moment the states of Europe are carving up Africa as they carved up America in the eighteenth century. They set about the process ten years ago with the most commendable deliberation, and with an attempt to establish rules of order for the process; but they are already snarling and growling at each other over the process, like hungry tigers over their prey. Germany and Italy, the two latest colonizers and the two whose domestic burdens and conditions fit them least for colonial enterprise, are the most eager and rapacious of all. The notion is that colonies are glory. The truth is that colonies are burdens—unless they are plundered, and then they are enemies. Russia is spreading her control over central Asia, although the internal cohesion of her empire is so weak that it will probably break in pieces under any great strain. France, after enormous losses in Tonkin, has just conquered Madagascar and joined England in carving up Siam.

The confusion between the economic use and the political jurisdiction is one of the strongest and most mischievous with which we have to deal. The best thing which could happen, from our point of view, is that England should "grab" all the land on the globe which is not owned by some first-class power. She would govern it all well, on the most enlightened and liberal principles, and we could all go to it for pleasure or gain as our interests might dictate. She would then have all the trouble, care, and responsibility, and we should all share the advantages. If there is a gold mine in Guiana, and if England gets the political jurisdiction of it, the English nation or exchequer will not get a grain of gold from the mine; if Englishmen get some of it, they can only do so by going to the mine and digging as individuals. Individuals of any other nationality can go there and do the same; if any Americans want to go there, they will undoubtedly have better chances if the civil jurisdiction of the district is English than if it is Venezuelan. . . .

Now let us not exaggerate, especially by ignoring what is sound and true in the old doctrines. Our own contests with Spain in Florida and Louisiana were unavoidable; she was not competent to govern her dependencies in a way to make them safe neighbors; she did not fulfill her duties in international law and comity. In Louisiana she held the mouth of the Mississippi River and tried to use her position to make the river and the Gulf of Mexico Spanish waters. Such pretensions were inadmissable. They rested on obsolete doctrines. She did not accept or fulfil the duties which would have devolved upon her in consistency with her own doctrines. Her claims were based on abstract rights which she alleged and which, if they had been admitted, would have been purely dogmatic. They did not rest on facts, or relations, or an adjustment of mutual interests; and they were not maintained with due responsibility such as must always go with a claim of right. The case was one, therefore, in which a civilized state of inferior rank could not maintain its hold on territory against a civilized state of higher rank. It was only another phase of the case presented by uncivilized tribes which try to hold territory against civilized colonists. There is, therefore, some truth to be admitted in the doctrine of "manifest destiny," although the doctrine is, like most doctrines in politics, a glib and convenient means of giving an appearance of rationality to an exercise of superior force. The truth in the doctrine is that an incompetent holder will not be able, as a matter of fact and in the long run, to maintain possession of territory when another nation which will develop it according to its capacity is ready to take it. A contemporary instance is furnished by the Transvaal, where the Boers certainly cannot maintain their independence and authority unless they prove themselves competent to maintain such civil institutions as are adequate to further the development of the territory.

Furthermore, civilized nations may find themselves face to face with the necessity of assuming the jurisdiction over territory occupied by uncivilized people, in order to police it and give local peace, order, and security, so that industry and commerce may be prosecuted there. The European nations now have this necessity in Africa. The fact remains, however, that the use of the land for production and the political jurisdiction of the territory are two entirely different things. What men want is to get at the land so as to till it and otherwise use it for industrial purposes; the political jurisdiction is a burden which is just so much of a drawback from the gain of using the land. If the industrial use could be got without taking the political jurisdiction, it would be far better. In other words, if the natives of any territory could maintain the customs and institutions which are necessary in order that peaceful industry and commerce may go on, that is a state of things which is far more desirable than that there should be any supersession of the native authority by any civilized state. The latter step is an irksome and harmful necessity for the state which makes it. . . .

There is another view of the political organization of the globe which we had supposed to be already well on towards realization. . . . It is the view of the states of the globe as forming a great family of nations, united by a growing body of international law, creating institutions as they are needed to regulate international relations, bound together in community of interest by free commerce, communicating to one another the triumphs won by each in science and art, sharing their thoughts by a common literature in which the barriers of language are made as little effectual as possible, and thus creating one society of the enlightened nations independent of state boundaries. Such an idea need only be expressed to show that it is the only conception of the relations of nations to each other which fits the enlightenment of our day. It is not in the least an ideal or a dream. It is only a construction of facts such as our international law already recognizes and rests upon. It does not preclude war between these nations, for nothing can preclude war; but it reduces the chances of it by extending the sway of reason and introducing into international relations ideas and institutions with which all enlightened nations are already familiar. Such a conception of international relations does not quench earth hunger. Nothing can quench that; for, as we have seen, it is the impulse which drives the human race to enter upon and enjoy its patrimony, the earth; but such a conception of the civilized races of the world in their relation to each other would bring into a clear light the difference between the extension of industry and commerce on the one side and political aggrandizement on the other. This distinction is no new thing; it is recognized and acted upon by all the most enlightened economists, publicists, and statesmen in the world. Neither is there anything new in the view of history and of the conflicts of policy which have here been presented; but if that view is true, then the Monroe Doctrine, or the doctrine of the dual political organization of the nations of the earth, is a barbaric stumbling-block in the way of enlightened international policy.

(From *Earth Hunger and Other Essays*, New Haven, 1913, pp. 31, 43-45, 51-52, 53-55, 62-63)

WILLIAM GRAHAM SUMNER, "The Fallacy of Territorial Extension," 1896

Territorial aggrandizement enhances the glory and personal importance of the man who is the head of a dynastic state. The fallacy of confusing this with the greatness and strength of the state itself is an open pitfall close at hand. It might seem that a republic, one of whose chief claims to superiority over a monarchy lies in avoiding the danger of confusing the king with the state, ought to be free from this fallacy of national greatness, but we have plenty of examples to prove that the traditional notions are not cut off by changing names and forms.

The notion that gain of territory is gain of wealth and strength for the state, after the expedient size has been won, is a delusion. . . .

It is said that the boundary between Alaska and British America runs through a gold field, and some people are in great anxiety as to who will "grab" it. If an American can go over to the English side and mine gold there for his profit, under English laws and jurisdiction, and an Englishman can come over to the American side and mine gold there for his profit, under American laws and jurisdiction, what difference does it make where the line falls? The only case in which it would make any difference is where the laws and institutions of the two states were not in equal stages of enlightenment.

This case serves to bring out distinctly a reason for the old notion of territorial extension which is no longer valid. In the old colonial system, states conquered territories or founded colonies in order to shut them against all other states and to exploit them on principles of subjugation and monopoly. It is only under this system that the jurisdiction is anything but a burden.

If the United States should admit Hawaii to the Union, the Fiscus of the former state would collect more taxes and incur more expenses. The circumstances are such that the latter would probably be the greater. The United States would not acquire a square foot of land in property unless it paid for it. Individual Americans would get no land to till without paying for it and would win no products from it except by wisely expending their labor and capital on it. All that they can do now. So long as there is a government on the islands, native or other, which is competent to guarantee peace, order, and security, no more is necessary, and for any outside power to seize the jurisdiction is an unjustifiable aggression. That jurisdiction would be the best founded which was the most liberal and enlightened, and would give the best security to all persons who sought the islands upon their lawful occasions. The jurisdiction would, in any case, be a burden, and any state might be glad to see any other state assume the burden, provided that it was one which could be relied upon to execute the charge on enlightened principles for the good of all. The best case is, therefore, always that in which the resident population produce their own state by the institutions of self-government.

What private individuals want is free access, under order and security, to any part of the earth's surface, in order that they may avail themselves of its natural resources for their use, either by investment or commerce. If, therefore, we could have free trade with Hawaii while somebody else had the jurisdiction, we should gain all the advantages and escape all the burdens. The Constitution of the United States establishes absolute free trade between all parts of the territory under its jurisdiction. A large part of our population was thrown into indignant passion because the Administration rejected the annexation of Hawaii, regarding it like the act of a man who refuses the gift of a farm. These persons were generally those who are thrown into excitement by any proposition of free trade. They will not, therefore, accept free trade with the islands while somebody else has the trouble and burden of the jurisdiction, but they would accept free trade with the islands eagerly if they could get the burden of the jurisdiction too.

Canada has to deal with a race war and a religious war, each of great virulence, which render governmental jurisdiction in the Dominion difficult and hazardous. If we could go to Canada and trade there our products for those of that country, we could win all for our private interests which that country is able to contribute to the welfare of mankind, and we should have nothing to do with the civil and political difficulties which harass the government. We refuse to have free trade with Canada. Our newspaper and congressional economists prove to their own satisfaction that it would be a great harm to us to have free trade with her now, while she is outside the jurisdiction under which we live; but, within a few months, we have seen an eager impulse of public opinion toward a war of conquest against Canada. If, then, we could force her to come under the same jurisdiction, by a cruel and unprovoked war, thus bringing on ourselves the responsibility for all her civil discords and problems, it appears to be believed that free trade with her would be a good thing.

The case of Cuba is somewhat different. If we could go to the island and trade with the same freedom with which we can go to Louisiana, we could make all the gains, by investment and commerce, which the island offers to industry and enterprise, provided that either Spain or a local government would give the necessary security, and we should have no share in political struggles there. It may be that the proviso is not satisfied, or soon will not be. Here is a case, then, which illustrates the fact that states are often forced to extend their jurisdiction whether they want to do so or not. Civilized states are forced to supersede the local jurisdiction of uncivilized or half-civilized states, in order to police the territory and establish the necessary guarantees of industry and commerce. It is idle to set up absolute doctrines of national ownership in the soil which would justify a group of population in spoiling a part of the earth's surface for themselves and everybody else. The island of Cuba may fall into anarchy. If it does, the civilized world may look to the United States to take the jurisdiction and establish order and security there. We might be compelled to do it. It would, however, be a great burden and possibly a fatal calamity to us. Probably any proposition that England should take it would call out a burst of jingo passion against which all reasoning would be powerless. We ought to pray that England would take it.

She would govern it well, and everybody would have free access to it for the purposes of private interest, while our Government would be free from all complications with the politics of the island. If we take the jurisdiction of the island, we shall find ourselves in a political dilemma, each horn of which is as disastrous as the other: either we must govern it as a subject province, or we must admit it into the Union as a state or group of states. Our system is unfit for the government of subject provinces. They have no place in it. They would become seats of corruption, which would react on our own body politic. If we admitted the island as a state or group of states, we should have to let it help govern us. The prospect of adding to the present senate a number of Cuban senators, either native or carpet-bag, is one whose terrors it is not necessary to unfold. Nevertheless it appears that there is a large party which would not listen to free trade with the island while any other nation has the jurisdiction of it, but who are ready to grab it at any cost and to take free trade with it, provided that they can get the political burdens too.

(From *War and Other Essays*, New Haven, 1911, pp. 286-290)

JOHN T. MORGAN, "The Territorial Expansion of the United States," 1898

The enlargement of our possessions in those countries that are outside of the grand sweep of the geographical lines of the Western Hemisphere, with its associated groups of islands, and are not naturally within the influence or control of the American people, would be attended with difficulties that are not found to exist within those limits. They are serious difficulties, and are to be weighed only with reference to some national duty, or necessity, such as the defense of our country, or the protection of our commerce. The aggrandizement of foreign conquest or the natural pride we may feel in the display of great forces in warfare, or in the accumulation of wealth, or of great influence in statecraft, would not justify the expansion of our borders to include territory in Europe, Asia or Africa. . . .

In the Philippines and the Carolines, where the unnatural disseverance of the people into distinct communities through the rule of the Spaniard is proven by the fact that they are so estranged from each other that more than 100 dialects are found among eight million people, their reunion as one family is possible only through some force inherent in the people which will be developed when peace is secured to them and freedom of thought and action are protected. . . .

If we should annex them as we have extended our borders over the Indian tribes, and rule them without permitting them to participate in the government, as we have done in the case of the Indians, they would be in better condition, it is true, than they are under Spanish rule; but they would ultimately perish, as the Indians are passing out. The influence upon our race of holding such people in political subjugation would be paralyzing to the energies and the noble aspirations that should always characterize the race called Anglo-Saxon.

We tried the institution of slavery in the actual and physical control of an inferior race and, while it lifted up the negro to a state of civilization far above that of his family in Africa and was, in that sense and in the Christian sense, the greatest missionary work that was ever done, it reacted upon our people with a degrading effect, and so disturbed our social organism, and so excited political jealousies, that we were plunged into a fratricidal war, from which we survived with a loss of life and property that is almost incomprehensible.

The political slavery of the inhabitants of any of the islands that we may occupy, would possibly entail evils upon our home Government of a like kind, in the outcome. The most we can do for the advancement of those people, is to secure peace and liberty of action to them; as the three great Powers are endeavoring to do in the Samoan Islands. If the United States, alone, were conducting this experiment in Samoa, the results would be more beneficial to those people, but so far they are not very satisfactory.

To take the Philippine Islands, for an illustration, it is a just expectation that the creation of a military station at a suitable port in Luzon Island would guarantee that group of islands against foreign interference and internecine warfare, and would give them an opportunity to adopt such political institutions as they prefer, under the right of local self-government. In such a course we would not assume sovereignty over them, but we would exert an influence upon them that would prevent them from disturbing our possessions, and would serve to protect them in turn, from foreign and domestic disturbances. Such territorial expansion is neither colonization nor conquest, in any political sense; and it is not more foreign to our just and necessary national policy than is commerce, or the freedom of the seas.

Our national vessels on the high seas, wherever they may go, are within the sovereign jurisdiction of the United States, and their decks and rightful seaway are liked to American soil as to their rights and responsibilities, and as to our duty to care for them. If they are sailing craft, the winds that propel them are a necessary part of their freedom of the seas. If they are steamers, we can extend our sovereignty, by legitimate means, to secure for them coaling stations and harbors of refuge, to be held in our own right, without a dangerous expansion of our borders, or of our political dominion. The present war is likely to result in our possession of places that are of great value to our legitimate commerce. They have, indeed, been thrust upon us by the necessary strategy of warfare, and are ours, rightfully, under the laws of nations. We would be wanting in duty to our people concerned in commerce—and none of them are without interest in this branch of our national enterprise—if we failed to secure for them the advantages of projected coaling stations at Manila, and at San Juan, in Porto Rico. This national duty is plain; and it is also true that coal is now more important than the winds as the motive power of commerce and war-ships.

If these obvious advantages to our country are acquired as the incidents of a just war, not waged for conquest, we cannot yield them without self-reproach; if we refuse to accept them it will be because we fear the effect upon our country of any expansion of our possessions beyond the limits of this continent. Such apprehensions are born of idle and unworthy fears, and they will relegate a progressive and competitive nation striving for the rewards of peaceful industry and the glory of a higher development, to the conditions of stagnant and fruitless cumberers of the earth. If an American cannot successfully conduct commerce pursuits on the high seas, under the flag of his country, and find protection and safety on all the important lines of navigation, our posterity will be led to regret that their fathers had not bequested to them the greater benefits that our race have secured under the British flag. No just reason can be given for a monastic policy which will shut up the energies of our people within a fixed limit, and compel them to trade within our present territory. This cannot be done without destroying the genius of our people.

If, indeed, we are freemen at home, there is the greater reason why we should have the largest liberty and the greatest security in trade and intercourse with other countries. This can be accomplished, in any part of the world, without annexing territory in countries that are outside the American sphere, and we should not hesitate to improve the opportunities that the war with Spain have placed within our reach, by acquiring military outposts and harbors of refuge for the protection of our commerce, and making them strong for defensive purposes.

(From *The Independent,* July 7, 1898, L, 10-12)

RICHARD OLNEY, "International Isolation of the United States," 1898

What is meant by the phrase "international isolation" as thus used is this. The United States is certainly now entitled to rank among the great Powers of the world. Yet, while its place among the nations is assured, it purposely takes its stand outside the European family circle to which it belongs, and neither accepts the responsibilities of its place nor secures its advantages. It avowedly restricts its activities to the American continents and intentionally assumes an attitude of absolute aloofness to everything outside those continents. This rule of policy is not infrequently associated with another which is known as the Monroe Doctrine—as if the former grew out of the Monroe Doctrine or were, in a sense, a kind of consideration for that doctrine, or a sort of complement to it. In reality the rule of isolation originated and was applied many years before the Monroe Doctrine was proclaimed. No doubt consistency requires that the conduct toward America which America expects of Europe should be observed by America toward Europe. Nor is there any more doubt that such reciprocal conduct is required of us not only by consistency but by both principle and expediency. The vital feature of the Monroe Doctrine is that no European Power shall forcibly possess itself of American soil and forcibly control the political fortunes and destinies of its people. Assuredly America can have no difficulty in governing its behavior toward Europe on the same lines.

Tradition and precedent are a potent force in the New World as well as in the Old and dominate the counsels of modern democracies as well as those of ancient monarchies. The rule of international isolation for America was formulated by Washington, was embalmed in the earnest and solemn periods of the Farewell Address, and has come down to succeeding generations with all the immense prestige attaching to the injunctions of the Father of his Country and of the statesmen and soldiers who, having first aided him to free the people of 13 independent communities, then joined him in the even greater task of welding the incoherent mass into one united nation. The Washington rule, in the sense in which it has been commonly understood and actually applied, could hardly have been adhered to more faithfully if it had formed part of the text of the Constitution. But there can be no question that such common understanding and practical application have given an extension to the rule quite in excess of its terms as well as of its true spirit and meaning. . . .

Now what is it that these utterances enjoin us not to do? What rule of abstinence do they lay down for this country? The rule is stated with entire explicitness. It is that this country shall not participate in the ordinary vicissitudes of European politics and shall not make a permanent alliance with any foreign power. It is coupled with the express declaration that extraordinary emergencies may arise to which the rule does not apply, and that when they do arise temporary alliances with foreign powers may be properly resorted to. Further, not only are proper exceptions to the rule explicitly recognized, but its author, with characteristic caution and wisdom, carefully limits the field which it covers by bounds which in practice are either accidentally or intentionally disregarded. For example, it cannot be intermeddling with the current course of European politics to protect American citizens and American interests wherever in the world they may need such protection. It cannot be intermeddling to guard our trade and commerce and to see to it that its natural development is not fraudulently or forcibly or unfairly arrested. . . .

Doubtless, whatever our rights, it would be folly to contend against a united Europe. Doubtless also, as we fence out all the world from our home markets, we ought not to count upon finding any nation to aid us in making the trade with China open to us as to all other nations on equal terms. It is conceivable, however, that such an ally might be found, and if it were found and the alliance were reasonably sure to attain the desired end at not disproportionate cost, there could not be two opinions as to its propriety. An illustration drawn from actual facts may be more impressive than any founded upon the conjecture of press correspondents. In 1884, most, if not all of the Powers of Europe being then engaged in extending their sovereignty over portions of the African continent, Germany and France cooperated in calling a general Conference at Berlin, and among the Powers invited included the United States, partly no doubt because of our peculiar relation to the Republic of Liberia and partly because of our present and prospective interest in trade with Africa. The declared objects of the Conference were briefly, first, freedom of commerce at the mouth and in the valley of the Congo; second, free navigation of the Congo and Niger rivers; and third, definition of the characteristics of an effective occupation of territory—it being understood that each power reserved the right to ratify or not to ratify the results of the Conference. Our government, finding nothing in the objects of the Conference that was not laudable, accepted the invitation. The Conference took place, this country being represented by our minister to Germany, who acquitted himself with distinguished ability. Indeed, not only did the Conference accomplish the general purposes named in the invitations to it, but, owing to the special initiative of the United States minister, the area of territory covered was largely extended, propositions were adopted for the neutralization of the region in case of war between the Powers interested and for mediation and arbitration between them before an appeal to arms, and instead of taking the form of a treaty the results of the Conference were embodied in a declaration called the "General Act of the Berlin Conference." Nevertheless, though signed by all the other parties to the Conference, and though we are so largely responsible for its provisions, the Act still remains without the signature of the United States. It was antagonized by reso-

lutions in the House of Representatives because of its supposed conflict with the rule of the Farewell Address. . . .

Political isolation may in a special case coexist with entire freedom
of commercial intercourse—as where a country is weak and small and
its resources, natural and artificial, are too insignificant to excite jealousy. Such was the case with the United States immediately after the
war of independence, when its inhabited territory consisted of a strip
of Atlantic seaboard and its people numbered less than four million
souls. But a policy of political isolation for a continental Power, rapidly
rising in population, wealth, and all the elements of strength, and able
to cope with the foremost in the struggle for the trade of the world,
naturally fosters, if it does not entail, a policy of commercial isolation,
also. The two policies are naturally allied in spirit and in the underlying considerations which can be urged in their defense, and being
once adopted render each other mutual support. Political isolation deliberately resolved upon by a great Power denotes its self-confidence
and its indifference to the opinion or friendship of other nations; in
like manner the commercial isolation of such a Power denotes its
conviction that in matters of trade and commerce it is sufficient unto
itself and need ask nothing of the world beyond. In the case of the
United States, the policy of political seclusion has been intensified by
a somewhat prevalent theory that we are a sort of chosen people;
possessed of superior qualities natural and acquired; rejoicing in superior institutions and superior ideals; and bound to be careful how we
connect ourselves with other nations lest we get contaminated and de-
teriorate. This conception of ourselves has asserted itself in opposition
to international arrangements even when, as in the case of the "General
Act of the Berlin Conference" already referred to, the only object and
effect were to open a new region to commerce and to give our merchants
equal privileges with those of any other country. We accept the privileges
but at the same time decline to become a party to the compact which
secures them to us as to all nations. . . . Do we want the same rights and
facilities of trade in Chinese ports and territory that are accorded to the
people of any other country? We loudly hark Great Britain on to the
task of achieving that result, but come to the rescue ourselves with
not a gun, nor a man, nor a ship, with nothing but our "moral sup-

port." But, not to tarry too long on details, what are the general results of these twin policies—of this foreign policy of thorough isolation combined with a domestic policy of thorough protection? So far as our foreign relations are concerned, the result is that we stand without a friend among the great Powers of the world and that we impress them, however unjustly, as a nation of sympathizers and swaggerers—without purpose or power to turn our words into deeds and not above the sharp practice of accepting advantages for which we refuse to pay our share of the price. . . .

Finally, one other feature of the situation must not be overlooked. While protectionism in this country has waxed mighty and all-pervading—our foreign shipping industry has languished and declined until it has become a subject of concern and mortification to public men of all parties. Time was when we built the best ships afloat and disputed the carrying trade of the world with Great Britain herself. Now we not only make no serious attempt to carry for other countries but are looking on while only about 12 per cent of our own foreign commerce embarks in American bottoms. What is the cause? Here are seven to eight thousand miles of coast, fronting Europe to the east and Asia to the west, belonging to 70 millions of people, intelligent, prosperous, adventurous, with aptitudes derived from ancestors whose exploits on the seas have resounded through the world and have not yet ceased to be favorite themes of poetry and romance. Why is it that such a people no longer figures on such a congenial field of action? The answer is to be found nowhere else than in the working of the twin policies we are considering—of commercial combined with political isolation. Under the former policy, when sails and timber gave way to steam and iron, protectionism so enhanced the cost of the essentials of steamship construction that any competition between American shipyards and the banks of the Clyde was wholly out of the question. Under the latter, the policy of political isolation, the public mind became predisposed to regard the annihilation of our foreign merchant service as something not only to be acquiesced in but welcomed. How could it be otherwise? If to stand apart from the group of nations to which we belong and to live to ourselves alone is the ideal we aim at, why should we not view with equanimity, or even with satisfaction, the loss of an industry which provides the connecting links between ourselves and the outer world? Though that loss was at first and for a considerable period in apparent accord with the popular temper, there is now a revulsion of sentiment, and a demand for the rehabilitation of our foreign merchant marine which seems to be both strong and general. . . .

A noted Republican statesman of our day, a protectionist though not of the extreme variety, is said to have remarked, "It is not an ambitious destiny for so great a country as ours to manufacture only what we can consume or produce what we can eat." But it is even a more pitiful ambition for such a country to aim to seclude itself from the world at large and to live a life as insulated and independent as if it were the only country on the foot-stool. A nation is as much a member of a society as an individual. Its membership, as in the case of an individual, involves duties which call for something more than mere abstention from violations of positive law. The individual who should deliberately undertake to ignore society and social obligations, to mix with his kind only under compulsion, to abstain from all effort to make men wiser or happier, to resist all appeals to charity, to get the most possible and enjoy the most possible consistent with the least possible intercourse with his fellows, would be universally condemned as shaping his life by a low and unworthy standard. Yet, what is true of the individual in his relations to his fellow men is equally true of every nation in its relations to other nations. In this matter, we have fallen into habits which, however excusable in their origin, are without present justification. Does a foreign question or controversy present itself appealing however forcibly to our sympathies or sense of right—what happens the moment it is suggested that the United States should seriously participate in its settlement? A shiver runs through all the ranks of capital lest the uninterrupted course of money-making be interfered with; the cry of "Jingo!" comes up in various quarters; advocates of peace at any price make themselves heard from innumerable pulpits and rostrums; while practical politicians invoke the doctrine of the Farewell Address as an absolute bar to all positive action. The upshot is more or less explosions of sympathy or antipathy at more or less public meetings, and, if the case is a very strong one, a more or less tardy tender by the government of its "moral support." Is that a credible part for a great nation to play in the affairs of the world? The pioneer in the wilderness, with a roof to build over his head and a patch of ground to cultivate and wife and children to provide for and secure against savage beasts and yet more savage men, finds in the great law of self-preservation ample excuse for not expending either his feelings or his energies upon the joys or the sorrows of his neighbors. But surely he is no pattern for the modern millionaire, who can sell nine tenths of all he has and give to the poor, and yet not miss a single comfort or luxury of life. This country was once the pioneer and is now the millionaire. It behooves it to recognize the changed conditions and to realize its great place among the Powers of the earth. It behooves it to accept the commanding position belonging to it, with all its advantages on the one hand and all its burdens on the other. It is not enough for it to vaunt its greatness and superiority and to call upon the rest of the world to admire and be duly impressed. Posing before less favored peoples as an exemplar of the superiority of American institutions may be justified and may have its uses. But posing alone is like answering the appeal of a mendicant by bidding him admire your own sleekness, your own fine clothes and handsome house and your generally comfortable and prosperous condition. He possibly should do that and be grateful for the spectacle, but what he really asks and needs is a helping hand. The mission of this country, if it has one, as I verily believe it has, is not merely to pose but to act—and, while always governing itself by the rules of prudence and common sense and making its own special interests the first and paramount objects of its care, to forego no fitting opportunity to further the progress of civilization practically as well as by eloquent words. There is such a thing for a nation as a "splendid isolation"— as when for a worthy cause, for its own independence, or dignity, or vital interests, it unshrinkingly opposes itself to a hostile world. But isolation that is nothing but a shirking of the responsibilities of high place and great power is simply ignominious. If we shall sooner or later—and we certainly shall—shake off the spell of the Washington legend and cease to act the role of a sort of international recluse, it will not follow that formal alliances with other nations for permanent or even temporary purposes will soon or often be found expedient. On the other hand, with which of them we shall as a rule practically cooperate cannot be doubtful. From the point of view of our material interests alone, our best friend as well as most formidable foe is that world-wide empire whose navies rule the seas and which on our northern frontier controls a dominion itself imperial in extent and capabilities. There is the same result if we consider the present crying need of our commercial interests. What is it? It is more markets for the consumption of the products of the industry and inventive genius of the American people. That genius and that industry have done wonders in the way of bursting artificial barriers of the "American system" and reaching the foreign consumer in spite of it. Nevertheless, the cotton manufacturing industry of New England bears but too painful witness to the inadequacy of the home market to the home supply—and through what agency are we so likely to gain new outlets for our products as through that of a Power whose possessions girdle the earth and in whose ports equal privileges and facilities of trade are accorded to the flags of all nations? But our material interests only point in the same direction as considerations of a higher and less selfish character. There is a patriotism of race as well as of country— and the Anglo-American is as little likely to be indifferent to the one as to the other. Family quarrels there have been heretofore and doubt- less will be again, and the two peoples, at the safe distance which the broad Atlantic interposes, take with each other liberties of speech which only the fondest and dearest relatives indulge in. Nevertheless, that they would be found standing together against any alien foe by whom either was menaced with destruction or irreparable calamity, it is not permissible to doubt. Nothing less could be expected of the close community between them in origin, speech, thought, literature, institutions, ideals—in the kind and degree of the civilization enjoyed by both. In that same community, and in that cooperation in good works which should result from it, lies, it is not too much to say, the best hope for the future not only of the two kindred peoples but of the human race itself. To be assured of it, we need not resort to *a priori* reasoning, convincing as it would be found, nor exhaust his- torical examples, numerous and cogent as they are. It is enough to point out that, of all obstacles to the onward march of civilization, none approaches in magnitude and obduracy "the scourge of war" and that the English and American peoples, both by precept and by example, have done more during the last century to do away with war and to substitute peaceful and civilized methods of settling international controversies, than all the other nations of the world combined have done during all the world's history. It is not too much to hope, let us trust, that the near future will show them making even more marked advances in the same direction, and, while thus consulting their own best interests, also setting an example sure to have the most important and beneficent influence upon the destinies of mankind.

(From *The Atlantic Monthly*, May, 1898, LXXXI, 577-588)

WHITELAW REID, "Territorial Expansion," 1899

The moment war was foreseen, the fleet we usually have in Chinese waters became indispensable, not merely, as before, to protect our trade and our missionaries in China, but to checkmate the Spanish fleet, which otherwise held San Francisco and the whole Pacific coast at its mercy. When war was declared, our fleet was necessarily ordered out of neutral ports. Then it had to go to Manila or go home. If it went home, it left the whole Pacific coast unguarded, save at the particular point it touched, and we should have been at once in a fever of apprehension, chartering hastily another fleet of the fastest ocean-going steamers we could find in the world, to patrol the Pacific from San Diego to Sitka, as we did have to patrol the Atlantic from Key West to Bar Harbor. Palpably this was to go the longest way around to do a task that had to be done in any event, as well as to demoralize our forces at the opening of the war with a manoeuvre in which our navy has never been expert—that of avoiding a contest and sailing away from the enemy! The alternative was properly taken. Dewey went to Manila and sank the Spanish fleet. We thus broke down Spanish means for controlling the Philippines, and were left with the Spanish responsibility for maintaining order there—responsibility to all the world, German, English, Japanese, Russian, and all the rest—in one of the great centres and highways of the world's commerce.

But why not turn over that commercial centre and the island on which it is situated to the Tagals? To be sure! Under 300 years of

Spanish rule barbarism on Luzon had so far disappeared that this commercial metropolis, as large as San Francisco or Cincinnati, had
sprung up and come to be thronged by traders and travellers of all
nations. Now it is calmly suggested that we might have turned it over
to one semi-civilized tribe, absolutely without experience in governing
even itself, much less a great community of foreigners, probably in a
minority on the island, and at war with its other inhabitants,—a tribe
which has given the measure of its fitness for being charged with
the rights of foreigners and the care of a commercial metropolis by
the violation of flags of truce, treachery to the living, and mutilation
of the dead, which have marked its recent wanton rising against the
Power that was trying to help it! . . .

It is quite true, as reported in what seemed an authoritative way
from Washington, that the Peace Commissioners were not entirely
of one mind at the outset, and equally true that the final conclusion
at Washington was apparently reached on the Commission's recommendation from Paris. As the cold fit, in the language of one of our
censors, has followed the hot fit in the popular temper, I readily take
the time which hostile critics consider unfavorable, for accepting my
own share of responsibility, and for avowing for myself that I declared
my belief in the duty and policy of holding the whole Philippine
Archipelago in the very first conference of the Commissioners in the
President's room at the White House, in advance of any instructions
of any sort. If vindication for it is needed, I confidently await the
future. . . .

It is said we are pursuing a fine method for restoring order, by pro-
longing the war we began for humanity in order to force liberty and
justice on an unwilling people at the point of the bayonet. The sneer
is cheap. How else have these blessings been generally diffused? How
often in the history of the world has barbarism been replaced by
civilization without bloodshed? How were our own liberty and justice
established and diffused on this continent? Would the process have
been less bloody if a part of our own people had noisily taken the
side of the English, the Mexican, or the savage, and protested against
"extreme measures"?

Some say a war to extend freedom in Cuba or elsewhere is right, and therefore a duty; but the war in the Philippines now is purely selfish, and therefore a crime. The premise is inaccurate; it is a war we are in duty bound to wage at any rate till order is restored—but let that pass. Suppose it to be merely a war in defence of our own just rights and interests. Since when did such a war become wrong? Is our national motto to be, "Quixotic on the one hand, Chinese on the other"? . . .

Again, we have superfine discussions of what the United States "stands for." It does not stand, we are told, for foreign conquest, or for colonies or dependencies, or other extensions of its power and influence. It stands solely for the development of the individual man. There is a germ of a great truth in this, but the development of the truth is lost sight of. Individual initiative is a good thing, and our institutions do develop it—and its consequences! There is a species of individualism, too, about a bulldog. When he takes hold he holds on. It may as well be noticed by the objectors that that is a characteristic much appreciated by American people. They, too, hold on. They remember, besides, a pregnant phrase of their Fathers, who "ordained this Constitution," among other things, "to promote the general welfare." That is a thing for which "this government stands" also; and woe to the public servant who rejects brilliant opportunities to promote it—on the Pacific Ocean no less than the Atlantic, by commerce no less than by agriculture or manufactures.

It is said the Philippines are worthless—have, in fact, already cost us more than the value of their entire trade for many years to come. So much the more, then, are we bound to do our duty by them. But we have also heard in turn, and from the same quarters, that every one of our previous acquisitions was worthless.

Again, it is said our continent is more than enough for all our needs, and our extensions should stop at the Pacific. What is this but proposing such a policy of self-sufficient isolation as we are accustomed to reprobate in China—planning now to develop only on the soil on which we stand, and expecting the rest of the world to protect our trade, if we have any? Can a nation with safety set such limits to its development? When a tree stops growing, our foresters tell us, it is ripe for the axe. When a man stops in his physical and intellectual growth he begins to decay. When a business stops growing it is in danger of decline. When a nation stops growing it has passed the meridian of its course, and its shadows fall eastward.

(From *American and English Studies,* New York, 1913, pp. 148-149, 150, 153, 158-159, 160-161)

WHITELAW REID, "Our Duty in the Philippines," 1899

Why mourn over our present course as a departure from the policy of the Fathers? For 100 years the uniform policy which they began and their sons continued has been acquisition, expansion, annexation, reaching out to remote wildernesses far more distant and inaccessible then than the Philippines are now—to disconnected regions like Alaska, to island regions like Midway, the Guano Islands, the Aleutians, the Sandwich Islands, and even to quasi protectorates like Liberia and Samoa. Why mourn because of the precedent we are establishing? The precedent was established before we were born. Why distress ourselves with the thought that this is only the beginning, that it opens the door to unlimited expansion? The door is wide open now, and has been ever since Livingston in Paris jumped at Talleyrand's offer to sell him the wilderness west of the Mississippi instead of the settlements eastward to Florida, which we had been trying to get; and Jefferson eagerly sustained him. For the rest, the task that is laid upon us now is not proving so easy as to warrant this fear that we shall soon be seeking unlimited repetitions of it. . . .

I have designedly left to the last any estimate of the material interests we serve by holding on in our present course. Whatever these may be, they are only a subordinate consideration. We are in the Philippines, as we are in the West Indies, because duty sent us; and we shall remain because we have no right to run away from our duty, even if it does involve far more trouble than we foresaw when we plunged into the war that entailed it. . . .

But the Constitution we revere was also ordained "to promote the general welfare," and he is untrue to its purpose who squanders opportunities. Never before have they been showered upon us in such bewildering profusion. Are the American people to rise to the occasion? Are they to be as great as their country? Or shall the historian record that at this unexampled crisis they were controlled by timid ideas and short-sighted views, and so proved unequal to the duty and the opportunity which unforeseen circumstances brought to their doors? The two richest archipelagoes in the world are practically at our disposal. The greatest ocean on the globe has been put in our hands, the ocean that is to bear the commerce of the twentieth century. In the face of this prospect, shall we prefer, with the teeming population that century is to bring us, to remain a "hibernating nation, living off its own fat—a hermit nation," as Mr. Senator Davis has asked? For our First Assistant Secretary of State, Mr. Hill, was right when he said that not to enter the Open Door in Asia means the perpetual isolation of this continent. . . .

Have you considered for whom we hold these advantages in trust? They belong not merely to the 75 millions now within our borders, but to all who are to extend the fortunes and preserve the virtues of the Republic in the coming century. Their numbers cannot increase in the startling ratio this century has shown. If they did, the population of the United States 100 years hence would be over 1200 millions. That ratio is impossible, but nobody gives reasons why we should not increase half as fast. Suppose that we do actually increase only one-fourth as fast in the twentieth century as in the nineteenth. To what height would not the 300 millions of Americans whom even that ratio foretells bear up the seething industrial activities of the continent! To what corner of the world would they not need to carry their commerce? What demands on tropical productions would they not make? What outlets for their adventurous youth would they not require? With such a prospect before us, who thinks that we should shrink from an enlargement of our national sphere because of the limitations that bound, or the dangers that threatened, before railroads, before ocean steamers, before telegraphs and ocean cables, before the enormous development of our manufactures, and the training of executive and organizing faculties in our people on a constantly increasing scale for generations?

(From *American and English Studies*, New York, 1913, pp. 188-189, 192-193, 195-196)

WILLIAM JENNINGS BRYAN, "The Issue in the
Presidential Campaign," 1900

The Philippine question is even plainer than the trust question, and
those who will be benefited by an imperial policy are even less in
number than those who may be led to believe that they would share
in the benefits of a gold standard or of a private monopoly. Here
again the Republicans dare not outline their policy. When the present
Congress was elected, in 1898, the treaty of peace had not yet been
signed. No definite issue was before the country, and the people
could not sit in judgment upon the purposes of the administration.

When the treaty was ratified, in February following, it was expressly
declared by several Republican Senators that the ratification of the
treaty did not determine the policy of the government, but merely
concluded the war with Spain. The McEnery resolution, adopted by
the votes of Republican Senators, declared that it was the sense of the
Senate that the Philippine Islands should never become an integral
part of the United States, but left the policy open for future consideration. The resolution was as follows:

> Resolved by the Senate and House of Representatives of the
> United States of America in Congress assembled, That by the
> ratification of the treaty of peace with Spain, it is not intended
> to incorporate the inhabitants of the Philippine Islands into
> citizenship of the United States, nor is it intended to perma-
> nently annex said islands as an integral part of the territory of
> the United States; but it is the intention of the United States
> to establish on said Islands a government suitable to the wants
> and conditions of the inhabitants of said islands, to prepare
> them for local self-government, and in due time to make such
> disposition of said islands as will best promote the interests of
> citizens of the United States and the inhabitants of said islands.

The nearest approach to a plan which has received any considerable
support among the Republicans is that outlined in the Spooner Bill,
which provides that:

When all insurrection against the sovereignty and authority of the United States in the Philippine Islands, acquired from Spain by the treaty concluded at Paris on the tenth day of December, eighteen hundred and ninety-eight, shall have been completely suppressed by the military and naval forces of the United States, all military, civil and judicial powers necessary to govern the said islands shall, until otherwise provided by Congress, be vested in such person and persons, and shall be exercised in such manner as the President of the United States shall direct for maintaining and protecting the inhabitants of said islands in the free enjoyment of their liberty, property and religion.

But this is far from definite. It means that, when the war is over (no one knows when that will be), the President is to do something (no one knows what), and is to keep at it (no one knows how long); and that Congress is to take some action (the nature of which no one can guess). Why the evasion? There can be but one reason for it, that the Republican leaders have decided upon a policy which they are not willing to outline, because they dare not risk the judgment of the American people in an open contest between the doctrine that governments rest upon force and the doctrine that governments derive their just powers from the consent of the governed.

If the Filipino is to be under our domination, he must be either citizen or subject. If he is to be a citizen, it must be with a view to participating ultimately in our government and in the making of our laws. Not only is this idea negated by the McEnery resolution, but it is openly repudiated by every Republican leader who has discussed the subject. If the Filipino is to be a subject, our form of government must be entirely changed. A republic can have no subjects. The doctrine that a people can be kept in a state of perpetual vassalage, owing allegiance to the flag, but having no voice in the government, is entirely at variance with the principles upon which this government has been founded. An imperial policy nullifies every principle set forth in the Declaration of Independence.

The Porto Rican tariff law illustrates this new doctrine. The flag is separated from the Constitution, and the Porto Ricans are notified that they must obey the laws made for them and pay the taxes levied upon them, and yet have no share in our Bill of Rights or in the guarantees of our Constitution. No monarch or tyrant in all history exercised more despotic power than the Republicans now claim for the President and Congress.

The theory that our race is divinely appointed to seize by force or purchase at auction groups of "inferior people," and govern them, with benevolent purposes avowed and with trade advantages on the side, carries us back to the creed of kings and to the gospel of force.

Lincoln condemned this doctrine with characteristic vigor in a speech made in 1858. He said that it was the old argument employed to defend kingcraft from the beginning of history; that "kings always bestride the necks of the people, not because they *desire* to do so, but because *the people are better off for being ridden."*

Those who advocate an imperial policy usually assert that the Filipinos are incapable of self-government. It might be a sufficient answer to quote the resolution of Congress declaring that "the Cubans are and of right ought to be free," and the report made by Admiral Dewey declaring that the Filipinos are far more capable of self-government than the Cubans. . . .

There are degrees of intelligence; some people can and do govern themselves better than others, and it is possible that the people living near the equator will never, owing to climatic conditions, reach the governmental standards of the temperate zone. But it is absurd to say that God would create the Filipinos and then leave them for thousands of years helpless, until Spain found them and threw her protecting arms around them; and it is equally absurd to say that Spain could sell us the right to act as guardians of a people whom she governed by force.

The purpose behind the imperial policy is the extension of trade. Franklin . . . denies that the securing or holding of trade is a cause for which men may justly spill each other's blood. The man who says that an imperial policy will pay must be prepared to place a pecuniary value upon the soldiers who have already lost their lives in the Philippines or have become insane from the effects of the climate, and upon the soldiers who will be sacrificed in future wars of conquest. The Republican party, which boasts that it sprang into existence in the defense of human rights, now coolly calculates the value of human life measured by Oriental trade. . . .

It will be noticed that Franklin also denied that trade could be profitably purchased and held by fleets and armies. History supports his contention. A nation never makes a profit out of a forcible extension of trade. Such a policy is defended by the few who make a great deal out of the trade, while the expenses of the war are borne by the taxpayers. There is no doubt that an imperial policy will be advantageous to army contractors, and to owners of ships who rent their vessels to the United States to carry live soldiers to the Philippine Islands and to bring dead soldiers back; and it may be advantageous to carpet-bag governors and to those who can secure good paying positions in the army, but it will be a constant drain upon the wealth producers. The amount already spent upon a war of conquest in a single year would almost construct the Nicaragua Canal; or, if used for the reclamation of arid lands in the West, it would furnish homes for more American citizens than would go to the Philippine Islands in a thousand years.

If an imperial policy is indorsed by the people, a large standing army will always be necessary. The same influences which lead to a war of conquest in the Philippines will lead to wars of conquest elsewhere, and an immense military establishment will not only become a permanent burden upon the people, but will prove a menace to the Republic.

One of the great objections to imperialism is that it destroys our proud pre-eminence among the nations. When the doctrine of self-government is abandoned, the United States will cease to be a moral factor in the world's progress. We cannot preach the doctrine that governments come up from the people, and, at the same time, practice the doctrine that governments rest upon brute force. We cannot set a high and honorable example for the emulation of mankind while we roam the world like beasts of prey seeking whom we may devour. . . .

While the Republican party has been evading a direct issue and trying to unload its mistakes upon Providence, the Democrats have urged a plain and simple remedy, viz., that we treat the Filipinos as we have promised to treat the Cubans. The Bacon resolution, which was defeated by the vote of the Vice-President just after the treaty was ratified, was supported by nearly every Democrat in the Senate, and was indorsed by a Democratic caucus in the House. It read as follows:

> Resolved, further, that the United States hereby disclaim any disposition or intention to exercise permanent sovereignty, jurisdiction, or control over said islands, and assert their determination, when a stable and independent government shall have been erected therein, entitled in the judgment of the government of the United States to recognition as such, to transfer to said government, upon terms which shall be reasonable and just, all rights secured under the cession by Spain, and to thereupon leave the government and control of the islands to their people.

Had this resolution been accepted by the Republicans at the time it was introduced, and acted upon by the administration, not a drop of blood would have been shed at Manila. Hostilities can be terminated at any moment by a declaration of this nation's purpose: first, to establish a stable government; second, to give the Filipinos their independence; third, to give them protection from outside interference while they work out their destiny. Such a declaration would be in harmony with American principles, American traditions and American interests. Such protection would be valuable to the Filipinos and inexpensive to us, just as protection to the South American republics has been of vital importance to them, while it has imposed no burden upon us.

Surely, the rapid development of plutocracy during the last few years will arouse the people to the dangers which threaten our Republic. The warning voice of history cannot longer be disregarded. No nation has ever travelled so far, in the same space of time, from democracy to plutocracy as has this nation during the last ten years. Foreign influence, described by Washington as "one of the most baneful foes of republican government," has been felt as never before. Fortunes have been made more suddenly than ever before. Corporate capital exerts an influence over government more potent than ever before. Money is more freely used than ever before to corrupt elections. . . .

If it is said that we are prosperous and that we live under the reign of law, let the reader review the lecture delivered by Dr. John

Lord, a Connecticut scholar, on Rome in the days of Marcus Aurelius. After describing the conditions which existed when "about two thousand people owned the whole civilized world," he says:

> But I cannot enumerate the evils which co-existed with all the boasted prosperity of the empire, and which were preparing the way for ruin—evils so disgraceful and universal that Christianity made no impression at all on society at large and did not modify a law or remove a single object of scandal.

And again:

> Is there nothing to be considered but external glories which appeal to the senses alone? Shall our eyes be diverted from the operation of moral law and the inevitable consequences of its violation? Shall we blind ourselves to the future condition of our families and our country in our estimate of happiness? Shall we ignore, in the dazzling life of a few favored extortioners, monopolists and successful gamblers, all that Christianity points out as the hope and solace and glory of mankind?

Instead of regarding the recent assault upon constitutional government—the attempted overthrow of American principles—as a matter of destiny, we may rather consider it as the last plague, the slaying of the first-born, which will end the bondage of the American people, and bring deliverance from the Pharaohs who are enthroning Mammon and debasing mankind.

(From *The North American Review*, June, 1900, CLXX, 754-771)

RICHARD OLNEY, "Growth of Our Foreign Policy," 1900

Though historians will probably assign the abandonment of the isolation policy of the United States to the time when this country and Spain went to war over Cuba, and though the abandonment may have been precipitated by that contest, the change was inevitable, had been long preparing, and could not have been long delayed. The American people were fast opening their eyes to the fact that they were one of the foremost Powers of the earth, and should play a commensurately great part in its affairs. Recognizing force to be the final arbiter between states as between individuals, and merit however conspicuous and well-founded in international law to be of small avail unless supported by adequate force, they were growing dissatisfied with an unreadiness for the use of their strength which made our representatives abroad less regarded than those of many a second or third class state, and left American lives and property in foreign countries comparatively defenseless. They had come to resent a policy and a condition of things which disabled the nation from asserting itself beyond the borders of the American continents, no matter how urgently such assertion might be demanded in the interests of civilization and humanity, and no matter how clearly selfish interests might coincide with generous impulses and with what might even be claimed to be moral obligations. They had begun to realize that their industrial and commercial development should not be checked by limitation to the demands of the home market but must be furthered by free access to all markets; that to secure such access the nation must be formidable not merely in its wants and wishes and latent capabilities but in the means at hand wherewith to readily exert and enforce them; and, as it could not hope to compass its ends without a sympathizer or friend among the nations, that it was imperative the United States should be ready to take any concerted action with other nations which its own special interests might require. In short, when our troubles with Spain came to a head, it had, it is believed, already dawned upon the American mind that the international policy suitable to our infancy and our weakness was unworthy of our maturity and our strength; that the traditional rules regulating our relations to Europe, almost a necessity of the conditions prevailing a century ago, were inapplicable to the changed conditions of the present day; and that both duty and interest required us to take our true position in the European family and to both reap all the advantages and assume all the burdens incident to that position. Therefore, while the Spanish war of 1898 is synchronous with the abandonment of its isolation policy by the United States, it was not the cause of such abandonment and at the most only hastened it by an inconsiderable period. So, while the Spanish war ended in the acquisition of Cuba by the United States, that result was neither unnatural nor surprising, but something sure to occur, if not in the year 1898, before many years, and if without war, then by a cession from Spain more or less compulsory in character. It may be thought at first blush that to speak of "the acquisition of Cuba by the United States" as a fact accomplished is inaccurate. But the objection is technical and the expression conveys the substantial truth, notwithstanding a resolution of Congress, which ill-advised and futile at the time of its passage, if now influential at all, is simply prejudicing the interests of Cuba and the United States alike. No such resolution can refute the logic of the undisputed facts or should be allowed to impede the natural march of events. To any satisfactory solution of the Cuban problem it is vital that Cuba's political conditions should be permanently settled. The spectacle now exhibited of a President and his Cabinet sitting in Washington with an appointee and sort of imitation President sitting with his Cabinet in the Antilles must have an end, the sooner the better, and will end when Congress ceases to ignore its functions and makes Cuba in point of law what she already is in point of fact, namely, United States territory. Were there to be a plebiscite on the subject, such a consummation would be favored by practically the entire body of the intelligence and wealth of the Island. Until it is reached, capital will hesitate to go there, emigration from this country will be insignificant, and Cuba will fail to enter upon that new era of progress and development, industrial, political, and social, which is relied upon to justify and ought to justify the substitution of American for Spanish control. . . .

It is true of states as of individuals—they never stand still, and if not going forward, are surely retrogressing. This evolution of the United States as one of the great Powers among the nations has, however, been accompanied by another departure radical in character and far-reaching in consequences. The United States has come out of its shell and ceased to be a hermit among the nations, naturally and properly. What was not necessary and is certainly of the most doubtful expediency is that it should at the same time become a colonizing Power on an immense scale. The annexation of the Hawaiian Islands need not now be taken into account and is to be justified, if at all, on peculiar grounds not possible to exist in any other case. But why do we find ourselves laboring under the huge incubus of the Philippines?

There has always been a popular impression that we drifted into the Philippines—that we acquired them without being able to help ourselves and almost without knowing it. But that theory—however in accord with the probabilities of the case—that theory, with all excuses and palliations founded upon it, is in truth an entire mistake. It is certain and has recently been declared by the highest authority that, having acquired by our arms nothing but a military occupation of the port and city of Manila, we voluntarily purchased the entire Philippine archipelago for 20 millions of dollars. . . . What duty did the United States have in the premises? The question of duty comes first—because, if there were any, it might be incumbent upon us to undertake its performance even at the sacrifice of our interests. What, then, was the call of duty that coerced us to take over the Philippine archipelago—that compelled us to assume the enormous burden of introducing order and civilization and good government into uncounted, if not uncountable, tropical islands lying thousands of miles from our coasts—that bound us to enter upon the herculean task of leading into the paths of "sweetness and light" many millions of people of all colors from the deepest black to the lightest yellow, of tongues as numerous and hopelessly diverse as those of the builders of the tower of Babel, and of all stages of enlightenment or nonenlightenment between the absolutely barbarous and the semi-civilized? It used to be said that our honor was involved—that having forcibly overthrown the sovereignty of Spain in the archipelago, we were bound in honor not to leave it derelict. But, as already noted, that proposition is completely disposed of by the official admission that we never held by conquest anything more than the city and harbor of Manila and that our title to everything else rests on purchase. The same admission disposes of the specious argument, a cheap resource of demagogy, that where the flag has once been hoisted it must never be taken down. But if, as now authoritatively declared, it had never been hoisted over more than the city and port of Manila, no removal of it from the rest of the archipelago was possible in the nature of things. If not bound in honor to buy the Philippines, how otherwise were we bound? A distinguished senator, on his return from England last summer, being asked what was thought there of our Philippine imbroglio, is said to have answered that the English were laughing in their sleeves at us. They were not laughing, it may be assumed, at our disasters. They were not merry, unquestionably, over our waste of millions of treasure and over our sacrifice through battle and disease of thousands of valuable lives. They would naturally rather applaud than scoff at our ambitions in the line of territorial extension. But British risibles, not too easily excited under any circumstances, must indeed have been adamant not to be moved by the justifications for our predicament vociferously urged by politicians and office-holders now especially prominent before the public. Does it appear or is it argued that the Spanish war was unnecessary—that the pear was ripe and ready to fall into our laps, without war and the killing of the reconcentrados, could we only have kept our heads and our tempers— that with a fair degree of tact and patience and common sense the Philippines might have been pacified—the astonishing answer is decla- mation about the beauties of the "strenuous life," the latest euphemism for war! Does it appear or is it claimed that no trade we are likely to have with the Philippines and China together is likely to compensate us for the enormous cost of first subjugating and afterwards defending and governing the Islands—an equally remarkable reply is that any such objections are shameful and unworthy; that we have a duty in the premises; and that whatever our wishes, or our interests or our sacrifices, we are under solemn obligation to carry the blessings of good government and civilization to the inhabitants of the Philippine archi- pelago! It is not easy to conceive of anything more baseless and more fantastic. As if war, under whatever alias, were not still the "hell" it was declared to be not by any apprentice to the trade but by one of the great commanders of the age; as if charity should not begin at home and he who fails to make those of his own house his first care were not worse than heathen; as if New York and Boston and all our cities did not have their slums and the country at large its mil- lions of suffering and deserving poor whose welfare is of infinitely greater importance to us than that of the Kanakas and Malays of the Orient, and whose relief would readily absorb all the energies and all the funds the United States can well spare for humane enterprises. No wonder our British kinsmen guffaw at such extraordinary justifications of our Philippine policy. The Britisher himself is as far as possible from indulging in any such sickly sentimentality. He quite understands that the first and paramount duty of his government is to himself and his fellow-subjects; that, as regards all outside of the British pale, whatever his government may do in the line of benevolence and charity is simply incidental and subsidiary. He fully realizes that if territory is annexed or control assumed of an alien race, it must be justified to the British nation by its promotion of the interests of the British Empire. If the transaction can be justified to the world at large as also in the interest of a progressive civilization—and it must be admitted that it often can be—so much the better. But the British policy is first and last and always one of selfishness, however superior in point of enlightenment that selfishness may be. It is so of necessity and in the nature of things— as must be the policy of every great Power. None can afford not to attend strictly to its own business and not to make the welfare of its own people its primary object—none can afford to regard itself as a sort of missionary nation charged with the rectification of errors and the redress of wrongs the world over. Were the United States to enter upon its new international role with the serious purpose of carrying out any such theory, it would not merely be laughed at but voted a nuisance by all other nations—and treated accordingly.

If not bound to buy the Philippines by any considerations of honor and duty, was it our interest to buy them?

Colonies may be greatly for the advantage of a nation. If it has a limited home territory and a redundant population, distant dependencies may afford just the outlet required for its surplus inhabitants and for the increase and diversification of its industries. It is manifest that no considerations of that sort are applicable in the case of the United States and the Philippines. Were our population ever so dense, it could not be drained off to the Philippines where the white laborer can not live. But the United States, far from having a crowded population to dispose of, has an enormous area of vacant land which for generations to come will be more than adequate to all the wants of its people. Our purchase of the Philippines can be justified, then, if at all, only by its effect in creating or extending trade and commerce with the Philippines and with China. What can be said for the purchase from that point of view?

On this subject the thick and thin supporters of the administration seek to dazzle our eyes with the most glowing visions. A soil as fertile as any on the globe needs but to be tickled with the hoe—to use Douglas Jerrold's figure—to laugh with abundant harvests of all the most desired tropical fruits. Minerals of all kinds are declared to abound everywhere—virgin forests of the choicest woods to be almost limitless in extent—while as for coal, it is solemnly asserted to be even dropping out of the tops of mountains. Nothing, in short, is too good or too strong for the defenders of the Philippine purchase to say of the natural resources of the Philippines, and with declamation on that single point, they usually make haste to drop the subject. They do not stop to tell us what we are to sell to a community whose members live on the spontaneous growth of their mother earth, and clothe themselves very much as did our first parents after the expulsion from Eden. They fail to tell us, further, with what labor the vaunted resources of the Islands are to be exploited, since the white laborer can not work there and the native will not. Shall we take the ground that what is bad for the United States is yet good enough for the Philippines and so legalize coolie immigration from China? Or, being just recovered from the bloodiest war of our time waged for the national life but caused and inspired by hatred of negro slavery, shall we now follow up our Philippine investment by adopting the system of quasi-slavery known as "Indentured Labor" and hire "black-birders," as they are called in Samoa, to "recruit" laborers in India or to steal or cajole negroes from among the outlying islands of the Pacific? Upon these as upon all the other difficulties which lead, not orators nor politicians, but businessmen and experts on the subject to declare that the Philippine trade will never repay the cost of acquisition, the friends of the Philippine purchase are discreetly silent. They do not, however, rest their case wholly, nor as a rule, even to any great extent, on the Philippine trade alone. They point to China—to its swarming millions and the immense markets which the breaking down of Chinese traditional barriers will afford to the nations of the West—and they triumphantly assert that here is to be found the more than sufficient justification for the Philippine purchase. The claim would be much exaggerated even if the Philippines could give us the entire Chinese market instead of simply letting us join in a neck and neck race for a share of it with every country of Europe. Be it assumed, however, that all that is said about the value of commerce with China—be it assumed, indeed, for present purposes that all that is said about the value of both the Philippine and the China trade—is fully borne out by the facts—what follows? That we were compelled to buy the Philippines in order to get our share? That is so far from being evident—is indeed so far from what seems to be the plain truth—that it is not too much to assert quite positively that we should have been in a better position to command our share of the Philippine and Chinese trade without the Philippines than with them. Chinese territory, it may be taken for granted, is not coveted by the most advanced of American jingoes. What they may come to in the future no one can predict, of course, but as yet no party and no section of any party in this country claims that, for the purposes of trade with China or for any other purpose, we should be one of the Powers to demand and extort territory or territorial rights in China. The efforts of the United States are limited—and wisely limited—to seeking for its ships and its merchants equal opportunities in China—to promoting in Chinese waters and on Chinese soil the policy known as the "open door." Is, then, the position of the United States, as insisting upon the "open door" in China, strengthened or weakened by its having the Philippine Islands on its hands? The administration has apparently memorialized European Powers on the ground of our legal rights to the "open door" under our treaties with China. But, if those Powers have been rightly appealed to, it must be because they have become paramount in China—because by conquest or unrestricted cession they have displaced China's sovereignty and substituted their own—in which case any observance by them of our treaty stipulations with China becomes matter of grace and favor purely. Our appeals are said to have brought satisfactory "assurances." But such "assurances" can hardly be regarded as definite obligations, nor as more than expressions of present views and intentions, nor as being more unchangeable than the views and intentions themselves. In these commercial days, governments do not give something for nothing—if they accord trade privileges, it is for value received or expected—and the official representative of the Czar in this country has already risen to explain as follows: "The extraordinary privileges for the importation of machinery and breadstuffs into Russia will of course not last forever. Americans understand the principle of the protective tariff too well to make lengthy explanation necessary.

When the Russian industries reach a stage where reasonable encourage-
ment will produce good results, of course the necessary protection
will be extended." We should indeed be credulous if we were to
believe that, when the time comes which the Russian Ambassador antici-
pates, either any "assurances" now given will prevent such customs
regulations by Russia as her own interest requires, or will lead her to
distinguish for our benefit between her Chinese possessions and her
territory generally. We can count upon the maintenance of the "open
door" in China, therefore, only if we can influence the Powers concerned in one of two ways—by making it their interest to grant it
through reciprocal concessions on our own part or by a manifest readiness to back our demand for it by such physical force as they will not
care to encounter. To the successful use of the first method, our Philippine possessions are a serious drawback if not an insuperable obstacle.
If we claim the "open door" of the Powers dominating China, how are
we to deny it to them in our own dependencies and especially in the
Philippines? One inconsiderate foreign office is already said to have
answered us by asking our intentions as to the Philippines, and might,
in view of the alleged vast extent of the Chinese markets, have not
impertinently inquired if some other American territory would not also
be opened to free trade. If the Philippines rather embarrass than help
us in securing the "open door" in China by amicable arrangement,
what is to be said upon the point of their enabling us to enforce it?
We are told that they place us in the "front door-yard" of the "Orient"
and, from that graphic figure of speech, are desired to infer and believe
that the entire Philippine archipelago was and is necessary to our possession of power and authority in the Pacific. But it might as well be
claimed that Gibraltar did not suffice for England's control of the
Mediterranean and that for that purpose she ought to have in addition
a large slice of Africa or of Spain. Assume to be true all that is said
of the value of trade with China—assume that, if we can not get it
by force—assume that, to use such force or be prepared to use it, we
must have a large navy which must be enabled to supply itself with
coal—assume all this—and there is still no satisfactory proof that we
had any occasion to buy the entire Philippine archipelago. Nothing,
indeed, follows except that it would have been wise for us to acquire
such part of the Philippines as was necessary to give us proper coaling

stations and an adequate naval base. If that and that only had been done, we should have been in a better position to secure and protect our interests in trade with China than we are with the Philippine load on our backs. We should have been more likely to reach our end by friendly negotiations because we should have seemed less aggressive; should have excited to a less degree the jealousies and the rivalries of foreign peoples; and should have had less difficulty with our anomalous attitude in demanding free trade with the dependencies of other countries while hampering free trade with our own by the severest restrictions. We should also have been stronger for accomplishing our object by force because, as compared with a proper naval base in the Philippines adequately supplied, fortified, and garrisoned, our possession of the entire Philippine group is a source of weakness rather than of strength. The Islands offer innumerable points of attack to any Power with a hostile animus. Yet we must always be prepared to defend each and all of them at all hazards and with all our resources—the Islands are ours as much as Massachusetts or Illinois—and not to maintain the integrity of American soil everywhere and against all comers, would deservedly expose us to universal contempt and derision. It follows, that whereas our trade with China would have been amply secured and protected by the enlarged navy we must and should have under any circumstances supplemented by an adequate naval base and coaling stations in the Philippines, the taking over of the whole archipelago enfeebles us for all purposes by the immense, remote, and peculiarly vulnerable area we must defend; by the large permanent army we must transport and maintain, not merely to prevent and deter aggression from without, but to hold down a native population thoroughly disaffected and resentful of the tactless and brutal policy hitherto pursued towards it; and by the tremendous drain on our resources which the civil and military administration of the Islands will inevitably entail.

Thus, adequate grounds for the purchase of the Philippines by the United States, for considering it to be demanded by duty, or honor, or interest, are not apparent. Nevertheless, however bad the blunder, the possession of sufficient legal power to commit us on the part of those in charge of the government for the time being must be conceded. Whether we want the Philippines or not, and whether we ought to have them or not, that we have got them is something not to be denied. They are our "old man of the sea"—with this difference in favor of Sindbad, that by intoxicating his monster he managed to get rid of him. It is tolerably certain there is no such way out for us, and that if intoxication is any element in the case at all, it must have supervened at the time our "old man of the sea" was foisted upon us.

The thing is done. We were an American Empire purely—and the United States, in taking its seat at the international council table and joining in the deliberations of civilized states, might have been in an ideal position, combining the height of authority and prestige with complete independence and with a liberty of action which would enable us to always make our own interests our first care and yet allow us, when permitted by those interests, to say a timely word or do a timely deed wherever civilization seemed to require. This possible—this natural—ideal position, an exercise of the treaty power by the national executive and senate has deprived us of. We are no longer an American Empire simply—we are become an Asiatic Empire also, environed by all the rivalries, jealousies, embarrassments, and perils attaching to every Power now struggling for commercial and political supremacy in the East, and starting the second century of national existence with all our energies and resources, which have proved no more than adequate to the good government of the white and black races of North America, pledged and mortgaged for the like services to be rendered by us to seven or eight millions of the brown men of the tropics. Nevertheless, as already stated, we are committed—the Philippines are ours—how we shall deal with them is a domestic question simply—so that, in this connection and at this time, what remains to be considered is the effect of this exact situation upon the future of our foreign relations. The United States now asserting itself not only as one of the great Powers of the world but as a Power with very large Asiatic dependencies—what consequent changes in respect of its foreign relations must reasonably be anticipated?

It goes without saying that the United States cannot play the part in the world's affairs it has just assumed without equipping itself for the part with all the instrumentalities necessary to make its will felt either through pacific intercourse and negotiation or through force. Its diplomatic agencies must, therefore, be greatly enlarged, strengthened, and improved, while a powerful navy, up to date in all points of construction, armament, general efficiency and readiness for instant service, becomes of equal necessity. Our Philippine possessions will not merely emphasize the urgent occasion for such innovations. They will make the innovations greater and more burdensome while at the same time compelling others which we could have done without. The Philippines inevitably make our navy larger than it would have to be without them—they inevitably enhance the extent and the quality and the cost of the diplomatic establishment with which we must provide ourselves. But besides aggravating the weight and the expense of the necessary burdens involved in our assuming our true place among the nations, the Philippines add burdens of their own. There will be no respectable government of the Islands until they are furnished with a large force of highly educated and trained administrators. Further, as already observed, were it not for the Philippines, we might have escaped the curse of any very large additions to our regular standing army. But the equipment required for our new international role need not be discussed at any length. We must have it—the need will be forced upon us by facts the logic of which will be irresistible—and however slow to move or indisposed to face the facts, the national government must sooner or later provide it. It is more important as well as interesting to inquire how the new phase of our foreign relations will affect the principles regulating our policy and conduct towards foreign states.

In dealing with that topic, it should be kept in mind that membership of the society of civilized states does not mean that each member has the same rights and duties as respects every subject-matter. On the contrary, the immediate interests of a nation often give it rights and charge it with duties which do not attach to any other. By common consent, for example, the right and duty of stopping the Spanish-Cuban hostilities were deemed to be in the United States on account of a special interest arising from Cuba's proximity to the United States and from the intimate relations of all sorts inevitably growing out of that proximity. So, though England is an insular Power, her home territory lies so near the European continent that the internal affairs of the European states directly interest her almost as much as if the English Channel were solid land. On the other hand, while the United States as regards Europe in general may also be regarded as an insular Power, its remoteness and separation from Europe by a great expanse of ocean make its interest in the internal affairs of European states almost altogether speculative and sentimental. Abstention from interference in any such affairs—in changes of dynasty, forms of government, alterations of boundaries and social and domestic institutions—should be and must be the rule of the United States for the future as it has been in the past. . . .

On similar grounds, the position we have assumed in the world and mean to maintain justifies us in undertaking to influence and enables us to greatly influence the industrial development of the American people. The "home market" fallacy disappears with the proved inadequacy of the home market. Nothing will satisfy us in the future but free access to foreign markets—especially to those markets in the East now for the first time beginning to fully open themselves to the Western nations. Hitherto, in introducing his wares and in seeking commercial opportunities of any sort in foreign countries, the American citizen has necessarily relied almost altogether upon his own unaided talents, tact, and enterprise. The United States as a whole has counted for little, if anything, in his favor—our notorious unreadiness for any exertion of our strength, divesting the government of all real prestige. In the markets of the Orient especially, American citizens have always been at a decided disadvantage as compared with those of European Powers. The latter impress themselves upon the native imagination by their display of warlike resources and their willingness to use them in aid not merely of the legal rights of their citizens but in many cases of their desires and ambitions as well. If the native government itself is in the market, it of course prefers to trade with the citizen of a Power in whose prowess it believes and whose friendship it may thus hope to obtain. If its subjects are the traders, they are affected by the same considerations as their government and naturally follow its lead in their views and their preferences. Obstacles of this sort to the extension of American trade can not but be greatly lessened in the future under the operation of the new foreign policy of the United States and its inevitable accompaniments. Our new interest in foreign markets can not fail to be recognized. Our claim to equal opportunities for our citizens and to exemption from unfriendly discrimination against them, will hardly be ignored if known to be backed by a present readiness and ability to make it good. "To be weak is miserable" and to seem weak, however strong in reality, often comes to about the same thing. Our diplomatic representatives, no matter how certain of the greatness of their country, have hitherto labored under the difficulty that nations to whom they were accredited, especially the Oriental nations, were not appreciative of the fact. That difficulty is unlikely to embarrass them in the future. They will, like the nation itself, cease to be isolated and of small consideration, and will speak and act with something of the same persuasiveness and authority as the representatives of European Powers. . . .

In undertaking any forecast of the future of our foreign relations, it is manifestly impracticable to attempt more than to note certain leading principles which, it would seem, must inevitably govern the policy of the United States. It is not rash to affirm in addition, however, that a consequence of the new international position of the United States must be to give to foreign affairs a measure of popular interest and importance far beyond what they have hitherto enjoyed. Domestic affairs will cease to be regarded as alone deserving the serious attention of Americans generally, who, in their characters, interests, and sympathies can not fail to respond to the momentous change which has come to the nation at large. Such a change will import no decline of patriotism, no lessening of the loyalty justly expected of every man to the country of his nativity or adoption. But it will import, if not for us, for coming generations, a larger knowledge of the earth and its diverse peoples; a familiarity with problems world-wide in their bearings; the abatement of racial prejudices; in short, such enlarged mental and moral vision as is ascribed to the Roman citizen in the memorable saying that, being a man, nothing human was foreign to him.

(From *The Atlantic Monthly*, March, 1900, LXXXV, 289-301)

THEODORE ROOSEVELT, "The Administration of the Island Possessions," 1902

The Spanish War itself was an easy task, but it left us certain other tasks which were much more difficult. One of these tasks was that of dealing with the Philippines. The easy thing to do—the thing which appealed not only to lazy and selfish men, but to very many good men whose thought did not drive down to the root of things—was to leave the islands. Had we done this, a period of wild chaos would have supervened, and then some stronger power would have stepped in and seized the islands and have taken up the task which we in such a case would have flinched from performing. A less easy, but infinitely more absurd course, would have been to leave the islands ourselves, and at the same time to assert that we would not permit any one else to interfere with them. This particular course would have combined all the possible disadvantages of every other course which was advocated. It would have placed us in a humiliating position, because when the actual test came it would have been quite out of the question for us, after some striking deed of savagery had occurred in the islands, to stand by and prevent the re-entry of civilization into them, while the mere fact of our having threatened thus to guarantee the local tyrants and wrong-doers against outside interference by ourselves or others would have put a premium upon every species of tyranny and anarchy within the islands.

Finally, there was the course which we adopted—not an easy course, and one fraught with danger and difficulty, as is generally the case in this world when some great feat is to be accomplished as an incident to working our national destiny. We made up our minds to stay in the islands—to put down violence—to establish peace and order—and then to introduce a just and wise civil rule accompanied by a measure of self-government which should increase as rapidly as the islanders showed themselves fit for it. It was certainly a formidable task; but think of the marvellously successful way in which it has been accomplished! The first and vitally important feat was the establishment of the supremacy of the American flag; and this had to be done by the effort of these gallant fellow Americans of ours to whom so great a debt is due—the officers and enlisted men of the United States regular and volunteer forces. In a succession of campaigns, carried on in unknown tropic jungles against an elusive and treacherous foe vastly outnumbering them, under the most adverse conditions of climate, weather, and country, our troops completely broke the power of the insurgents, smashed their armies, and harried the broken robber bands into submission. In its last stages, the war against our rule sank into mere brigandage; and what our troops had to do was to hunt down the parties of ladrones. It was not an easy task which it was humanly possible to accomplish in a month or a year; and therefore after the first month and the first year had elapsed, some excellent people said that it couldn't be done; but it was done. Month by month, year by year, with unwearied and patient resolution, our army in the Philippines did the task which it found ready at hand until the last vestige of organized insurrection was stamped out. I do not refer to the Moros, with whom we have exercised the utmost forebearance, but who may force us to chastise them if they persist in attacking our troops. We will do everything possible to avoid having trouble with them, but if they insist upon it it will come. Among the Filipinos proper, however, peace has come. Doubtless here and there sporadic outbreaks of brigandage will occur from time to time, but organized warfare against the American flag has ceased, and there is no reason to apprehend its recurrence. Our army in the islands has been reduced until it is not a fourth of what it was at the time the outbreak was at its height. . . .

At last, on the July 4th that has just passed—on the one hundred and twenty-sixth anniversary of our independence—it was possible at the same time to declare amnesty throughout the islands and definitely to establish civil rule over all of them, excepting the country of the Mohammedan Moros, where the conditions were wholly different. Each inhabitant of the Philippines is now guaranteed his civil and religious rights, his rights to life, personal liberty, and the pursuit of happiness, subject only to not infringing the rights of others. It is worth noting that during these three or four years under us the Philippine people have attained to a greater degree of self-government, that they now have more to say as to how they shall be governed, than is the case with any people in the Orient which is under European rule. Nor is this all. Congress has, with far-seeing wisdom, heartily supported all that has been done by the Executive. Wise laws for the government of the Philippine Islands have been placed upon the statute-books, and under those laws provision is made for the introduction into the Philippines of representative government, with only the delay absolutely necessary to allow for the establishment of definite peace, for the taking of a census, and the settling down of the country.

In short, we are governing the Filipinos primarily in their interest, and for their very great benefit. And we have acted in practical fashion—not trying to lay down rules as to what should be done in the remote and uncertain future, but turning our attention to the instant need of things and meeting that need in the fullest and amplest way. . . .

Nor should it be forgotten that while we have thus acted in the interest of the islanders themselves, we have also helped our own people. Our interests are as great in the Pacific as in the Atlantic. The welfare of California, Oregon, and Washington is as vital to the nation as the welfare of New England, New York, and the South Atlantic states. The awakening of the Orient means very much to all the nations of Christendom, commercially no less than politically; and it would be short-sighted statesmanship on our part to refuse to take the necessary steps for securing a proper share to our people of this commercial future. The possession of the Philippines has helped us, as the securing of the open door in China has helped us. Already the Government has taken the necessary steps to provide for the laying of a Pacific cable under conditions which safeguard absolutely the interests of the American public. Our commerce with the East is growing rapidly. Events have abundantly justified, alike from the moral and material standpoint, all that we have done in the Far East as a sequel to our war with Spain.

(From *The Works of Theodore Roosevelt,* New York, 1925, XVIII, 360-365)

III
The Challenges
Ahead

ONCE THE "New Manifest Destiny's" spokesmen began to see around the outer edges of those bothersome territorial snarls which had bunched up and constricted their thinking at the end of the war with Spain, they quickly shifted their full attention back to the main course ahead. Looming up just beyond were new obstacles and likely rivals. Basic to speculations about both were their assessments of the nation's growth to world stature, and the forces they believed would sustain its continued and steady economic expansion. The shape of obstacles ahead and the means to overcome them were all of a whole. "The lineage of our thoughts is unbroken. The nation that was in the making then," reasoned Woodrow Wilson, in a typical statement of their ideas, "was the nation which yesterday intervened in the affairs of Cuba, and to-day troubles the trade and the diplomacy of the world. . . ."

Another time, referring to the future course, Wilson had declared: "Our interests must march forward, altruists though we are: other nations must see to it that they stand off, and do not seek to stay us. . . ." More specifically, Wilson held that the United States required the kind of strong presidential leadership in the new century that it had called forth from the best of the Founding Fathers. Then as in the new era the most crucial tasks were to be centered in the management of foreign affairs. As fortune would have it, he received an exceptional opportunity to fill that very role in little more than a decade.

Of course no such chance came to Frederic Emory, or to Brooks Adams, or to Frank A. Vanderlip, but each did command a measure of influence over policy decisions in the political or economic life of the nation. In 1902 they all addressed the leadership community through leading periodicals of the day: From his desk in the State Department, Emory called attention to America's "New Horizon"; Adams described the features of the "New Empire"; and just back from Europe, Vanderlip reported on the "Commercial Invasion" of that Continent being carried forward by exports of United States products and manufactures. But none of these men tried to side-step or to minimize the danger spots they foresaw even amidst the encouraging developments surrounding America's recovery from the depression, its successful resolution of the war and the colonial dilemma, and the surprising expansion of its export trade.

A humorously written account of the impact made by the American "Invaders" appeared in England, but its intent was a serious warning to that country's manufacturers and foreign traders. Ray Stannard Baker, one of the most prolific writers in the Progressive Era, also pinpointed European reactions to the growth of American trade.

Like many others, Emory was disturbed that America's insistence upon maintaining prohibitive tariffs would bring down retaliations in force against the nation's trade. Adams called upon his fellow countrymen to update their ideas about economics and politics for the very good reason that America's ability to compete with its rivals in the world at large depended upon securing the greatest efficiency the United States could develop and maintain. Vanderlip had a similar concern about the social question at home, though his remedies varied considerably from those advocated by Adams.

Nearly all of these problems were related to the tariff question, or, more properly, to the question of some kind of tariff bargaining to match the agreements European nations had been accustomed to make between themselves and with areas producing raw materials. President William McKinley, the best-known champion of "Protectionism," had come to believe that this work extended to foreign trade. Hence he appointed John Kasson to make a beginning in that work as United States Reciprocity Commissioner. Robert P. Porter described the evolution of "Protectionism" in the 1890's, and Kasson himself later noted McKinley's own development in this direction.

As the new century began, American manufacturers subscribed to a whole series of celebrations or expositions which climaxed with the Louisiana Purchase Centennial in 1903. At all of these fairs the main theme sounded a call to greater foreign trade and exchange with all nations of the world. At one of these, the Buffalo Pan-American Exposition of 1901, President McKinley, in what turned out to be his "Last Public Utterance to the People," asserted that both Republicans and Democrats had to take a new look at the whole issue. The ancient (almost mythical) clash between protectionists and free traders was in fact no longer pertinent to the exigencies of the dawning era. McKinley and Mark Hanna had both worked on this speech which included these firm declarations: "The period of exclusiveness is past. The expansion of our trade and commerce is the pressing problem." If one would sell, he must also buy.

The "Kasson Treaties," as they were popularly known, never received the approval of the United States Senate. All kinds of unresolved divisions between raw materials producers and manufacturers, sectional divisions, and the power of certain blocs to surpass the needed one-third-plus-one vote contributed to their failure. Theodore Roosevelt witnessed this debacle and did not press the subject during his Administration. The new President also felt that the tariff was still a bread and butter party issue, although he believed it was also an anachronism. If left alone the tariff issue would cool off enough so that a future president could handle it without burning himself and his party.

So be it, wrote Brooks Adams; but if such a decision were made, if the Kasson policy or some other plan for reciprocity was not to be attempted, then the United States should arm itself and build warships for its navy to meet an inevitable challenge which could come from several nations in Europe. Those powerful and haughty powers would not willingly see themselves put in the shadow of this young colossus which suddenly bestrode the paths to raw materials sources and to the marketplaces of the world.

Senator Mark Hanna, meanwhile, was telling his colleagues in the lawmaking body of the need for federal subsidies for merchant ships. The United States had to provide facilities for its exporters, and, as seemed necessary, Congress must find the money to develop the Pacific trade routes.

And John Foord, one of the key leaders in the American Asiatic

Association, reviewing recent events in the Far East, made it quite plain that no matter what was done about reciprocity, the Russian advance in Manchuria had to be halted if American interests were to survive.

In the four years between 1901 and 1905, several decisions were made by American policy-makers with President Roosevelt leading the way: United States power and influence in the Pacific regions steadily grew, keeping pace with the activity of other nations. Still, Roosevelt was displeased that he could not meet the Russian challenge head on, instead of being restricted to diplomatic maneuvers. Japan's request that he mediate the end of the war between that country and Russia brought TR the sort of opportunity he had hoped for, however, and he eagerly used this chance to improve America's position in Asia. After securing pledges from the victorious but war-weary Japanese that they would implement the open door policy in areas freed from Russian domination in Manchuria, Roosevelt exerted his best efforts to play off the two so that the United States might also secure its share of the fruits of victory.

Japan's reluctance to accept limitations upon its ambitions in the Far East soon proved, however, as great an obstacle as the Russian bear had been, and the United States hurried to complete its Big Stick in the form of the Great White Fleet. Just as the fleet made a worldwide tour in the last years of Roosevelt's presidency, so had American economic expansion been launched on a world-wide scale—behind the aegis of the open-door policy.

More far-reaching matters were put in the works in these years as well: A fuse had been lighted under the tariff log jam which produced a series of explosions culminating with a big bang in the 1934 Reciprocal Trade Agreements Act. Ship subsidies were taken up by Woodrow Wilson when the pressures on American exporters at the outset of World War I offered his administration a chance to build a merchant fleet. The most difficult problem ahead proved to be the issue of America's relation to political alliances. Woodrow Wilson, once again, tried to move the nation into political councils at the end of the Great War, but as it had refused to follow McKinley's early advice on the tariff, so in 1919 it turned its back on another President's urgings. That step had to await another challenge and another war.

Woodrow Wilson, "Democracy and Efficiency," 1901

There is no masking or concealing the new order of the world. It is not the world of the eighteenth century, nor yet of the nineteenth. A new era has come upon us like a sudden vision of things unprophesied, and for which no polity has been prepared. Here is straightway a new frontage for the nations,—this frontage toward the Orient. Our almost accidental possession of the Philippines has put us in the very presence of the forces which must make the politics of the twentieth century radically unlike the politics of the nineteenth; but we must have taken cognizance of them and dealt with them in any event. They concern us as nearly as they concern any other nation in the world. They concern all nations, for they shall determine the future of the race. Fortunately, they have not disclosed themselves before we were ready. I do not mean that our thought was prepared for them; I do not mean that our domestic affairs were in such shape as to seem fairly well ordered, so that we might in good conscience turn from them as from things finished and complete, and divert our energies to tasks beyond our borders. I mean that this change in the order of the world came, so far as we are concerned, at the natural point in our national development. The matter is worth looking into.

There has been a certain singular unity in our national task, hitherto; and these new duties now thrust upon us will not break that unity. They will perpetuate it, rather, and make it complete, if we keep but our integrity and our old-time purpose true. Until 1890 the United States had always a frontier; looked always to a region beyond, unoccupied, unappropriated, an outlet for its energy, a new place of settlement and of achievement for its people. For nearly 300 years their growth had followed a single law,—the law of expansion into new territory. Themselves through all their history a frontier, the English colonies in America grew into a nation whose life poured still with strong tide along the old channel. Over the mountains on to the long slopes that descended to the Mississippi, across the great river into the plains, up the plains to the crowning heights of the Rockies, beyond the Rockies to the Pacific, slowly moved the frontier nation. England sought colonies at the ends of the earth to set her energy free and give vent to her enterprise; we, a like people in every impulse of mastery and achievement, had our own vast continent and were satisfied. There was always space and adventure enough and to spare, to satisfy the feet of our young men. . . .

No other modern nation has been schooled as we have been in big undertakings and the mastery of novel difficulties. We have become confirmed in energy, in resourcefulness, in practical proficiency, in self-confidence. We have become confirmed also, so far as our character is concerned, in the habit of acting under an odd mixture of selfish and altruistic motives. Having ourselves a population fit to be free, making good its freedom in every sort of unhampered enterprise, determining its own destiny unguided and unbidden, moving as it pleased within wide boundaries, using institutions, not dominated by them, we have sympathized with freedom everywhere; have deemed it niggardly to deny an equal degree of freedom to any race or community that desired it; have pressed handsome principles of equity in international dealings; have rejoiced to believe that our principles might some day make every government a servant, not a master, of its people. Ease and prosperity have made us wish the whole world to be as happy and well to do as ourselves; and we have supposed that institutions and principles like our own were the simple prescription for making them so. And yet, when issues of our own interest arose, we have not been unselfish. We have shown ourselves kin to all the world, when it came to pushing an advantage. Our action against Spain in the Floridas, and against Mexico on the coasts of the Pacific; our attitude toward first the Spaniards, and then the French, with regard to the control of the Mississippi; the unpitying force with which we thrust the Indians to the wall wherever they stood in our way, have suited our professions of peacefulness and justice and liberality no better than the aggressions of other nations that were strong and not to be gainsaid. Even Mr. Jefferson, philanthropist and champion of peaceable and modest government though he was, exemplified this double temper of the people he ruled. "Peace is our passion," he had declared; but the passion abated when he saw the mouth of the Mississippi about to pass into the hands of France. Though he had loved France and hated England, he did not hesitate then what language to hold. "There is on the globe," he wrote to Mr. Livingston at Paris, "one single spot the possessor of which is our natural and habitual enemy. The day that France takes possession of New Orleans seals the union of two nations, who, in conjunction, can maintain exclusive possession of the sea. From that moment we must marry ourselves to the British fleet and nation." Our interests must march forward, altruists though we are: other nations must see to it that they stand off, and do not seek to stay us. . . .

We did not of deliberate choice undertake these new tasks which shall transform us. All the world knows the surprising circumstances which thrust them upon us. Sooner or later, nevertheless, they would have become inevitable. If they had not come upon us in this way, they would have come in another. They came upon us, as it was, though unexpected, with a strange opportuneness, as if part of a preconceived plan for changing the world. Every man now knows that the world is to be changed,—changed according to an ordering of Providence hardly so much as foreshadowed until it came; except, it may be, to a few Europeans who were burrowing and plotting and dreaming in the mysterious East. The whole world had already become a single vicinage; each part had become neighbor to all the rest. No nation could live any longer to itself, the tasks and the duties of neighborhood being what they were. Whether we had had a material foothold there or not, it would have been the duty of the United States to play a part, and a leading part at that, in the opening and the transformation of the East. We might not have seen our duty, had the Philippines not fallen to us by the wilful fortune of war; but it would have been our duty, nevertheless, to play the part we now see ourselves obliged to play. The East is to be opened and transformed, whether we will or no; the standards of the West are to be imposed upon it; nations and peoples which have stood still the centuries through are to be quickened, and made part of the universal world of commerce and of ideas which has so steadily been a-making by the advance of European power from age to age. It is our peculiar duty, as it is also England's, to moderate the process in the interests of liberty: to impart to the peoples thus driven out upon the road of change, so far as we have opportunity or can make it, our own principles of self-help; teach them order and self-control in the midst of change; impart to them, if it be possible by contact and sympathy and example, the drill and habit of law and obedience which we long ago got out of the strenuous processes of

English history; secure for them, when we may, the free intercourse and the natural development which shall make them at least equal members of the family of nations. In China, of course, our part will be indirect, but in the Philippines it will be direct; and there in particular must the moral of our polity be set up and vindicated.

(From *The Public Papers of Woodrow Wilson*, New York, 1925, I, 402-405, 411-413)

WOODROW WILSON, "The Ideals of America," 1902

Not battles or any stirring scene of days of action, but the slow processes by which we grew and made our thought and formed our purpose in quiet days of peace, are what we find it hard to make real to our minds again, now that we are mature and have fared far upon the road. Our life is so broad and various now, and was so simple then; the thoughts of those first days seem crude to us now and unreal. We smile upon the simple dreams of our youth a bit incredulously, and seem cut off from them by a great space. And yet it was by those dreams we were formed. The lineage of our thoughts is unbroken. The nation that was making then was the nation which yesterday intervened in the affairs of Cuba, and today troubles the trade and the diplomacy of the world. . . .

This great pressure of a people moving always to new frontiers, in search of new lands, new power, the full freedom of a virgin world, has ruled our course and formed our policies like a Fate. It gave us, not Louisiana alone, but Florida also. It forced war with Mexico upon us, and gave us the coasts of the Pacific. It swept Texas into the Union. It made far Alaska a territory of the United States. Who shall say where it will end?

The census takers of 1890 informed us, when their task was done, that they could not longer find any frontier upon this continent; that they must draw their maps as if the mighty process of settlement that had gone on, ceaseless, dramatic, the century through, were now ended and complete, the nation made from sea to sea. We had not pondered their report a single decade before we made new frontiers for ourselves beyond the seas, accounting the 7,000 miles of ocean that lie between us and the Philippine Islands no more than the 3,000 which once lay between us and the coasts of the Pacific. No doubt there is here a great revolution in our lives. No war ever transformed us quite as the war with Spain transformed us. No previous years ever ran with so swift a change as the years since 1898. We have witnessed a new revolution. That little group of states, which 125 years ago cast the sovereignty of Britain off, is now grown into a mighty power. That little confederation has now massed and organized its energies. A confederacy is transformed into a nation. The battle of Trenton was not more significant than the battle of Manila. The nation that was 125 years in the making has now stepped forth into the open arena of the world. . . .

We have come to full maturity with this new century of our national existence and to full self-consciousness as a nation. And the day of our isolation is past. We shall learn much ourselves now that we stand closer to other nations and compare ourselves first with one and again with another. Moreover, the centre of gravity has shifted in the action of our federal government. It has shifted back to where it was at the opening of the last century, in that early day when we were passing from the gristle to the bone of our growth. For the first 26 years that we lived under our federal Constitution foreign affairs, the sentiment and the policy of nations oversea, dominated our politics, and our Presidents were our leaders. And now the same thing has come about again. Once more it is our place among the nations that we think of; once more our Presidents are our leaders.

(From *The Public Papers of Woodrow Wilson*, New York, 1925, I, 419-420, 425-426, 441)

FREDERIC C. EMORY, "Our New Horizon," 1902

In comparing the United States with the other Great Powers, we must also take into account the overwhelming superiority of our natural resources. There is no country in Europe which approaches us in variety or volume of products of the soil, the forest, the mine, and all the industrial nations are more or less dependent upon us for the raw material for their manufactures, as well as for food supplies. . . .

Given these natural advantages, with a busy, restless, inventive people, and it was inevitable that, sooner or later, the time would come when we should cease to be satisfied with merely domestic interests and would begin to look abroad for a wider exercise of our energies. The time came even before the Spanish war. We had long since reached the limit of continental expansion, except at the cost of gratuitous aggression upon our neighbors, Canada and Mexico. Although we were far from having occupied all our territory, in the sense of reducing it to tillage, and still had plenty of elbow room in the West, we were suffering from a sense of constraint, a vague feeling that we were not exerting ourselves to the full extent of our powers. For a long time we had been in the habit of regarding ourselves as a great people, but we felt that we were doing but little to impress this fact upon the rest of the world.

In the meantime we had unconsciously been equipping ourselves for the role we were destined to play. Our very absorption in the task of internal development, of the most effective utilization of our natural resources, of building up a vast fabric of industrial efficiency, was the best of all preparations for a triumphant entry upon the great world-stage of international competition. Economy of production as the result of cheap and abundant raw materials, the application of machinery and labor-saving tools to almost every form of mechanical effort, the invention of improved processes and methods of manufacture, and above all the superior industry, ingenuity and adaptability of our artisans and operatives, were gradually brought to a point of perfection which has thus far defied all rivalry or imitation. Without knowing it, we were fashioning the master key that was to unlock for us the markets of the world and thus provide a new channel for the national instinct of expansion, the national dream of greatness to be seen and admired of all.

As has frequently been remarked, it was this latent force, already at the point of eruption, which gave such momentum and energy to the war with Spain and controlled the final settlement of the terms on which peace was made. We were not in need of more territory, but commercial expansion had become a matter of pressing urgency if we were to advance along the existing lines of our accelerated industrial development. In other words, we were producing more than we could market at home, and if we wished to keep our factories going and our workmen fully employed it was evident we must seek new outlets abroad. It was not the mere greed of political aggrandizement that moved the great body of our people to accept and approve the territorial expansion resulting from the war with Spain, but the gradually widening perception of the fact that the results of the war were likely to contribute immensely to our commercial influence and prestige.

In espousing the cause of Cuba against Spain we were undoubtedly animated, to a very large extent, by indignation and sympathy with a people we believed to be cruelly oppressed, but underlying the popular sentiment which might have evaporated in time, with ameliorating changes in the Spanish policy, was the settled conviction that so long as Cuba remained a dependency of Spain our economic relations not only with that island but with the whole of the West Indies, and to a greater or less extent with all Latin America, would be impossible of adjustment on any safe or permanent basis. Cuba was in fact a stumbling block, a constant menace to the southward movement of our trade. To free her from the Spanish incubus was, therefore, a commercial necessity for us, and as we became more and more keenly alive to the importance of extending our foreign commerce, the impatience of our business interests at such obstruction was waxing so strong that, even had there been no justifying cause of an emotional kind, such as the alleged enormities of Spanish rule or the destruction of the *Maine,* we would doubtless have taken steps, in the end, to abate with the strong hand what was seen to be an economic nuisance.

But important and far-reaching as were the consequences of the Spanish war, it was but an incident of a general movement of expansion which had its roots in the changed requirements of an industrial capacity swollen far beyond our domestic powers of consumption. It was seen to be necessary for us not only to find foreign purchasers for our goods, but to provide the means of making access to foreign markets easy, economical and safe. Hence the rapidly augmenting popular interest in projects which had languished for years, for building up our ocean marine, for cutting an isthmian canal, for establishing better banking facilities in foreign countries, for the improvement of the consular service in order to make it a more efficient instrument of trade, for the modification of our tariff relations with the view to enlargement and greater freedom of exchange. However widely men may differ as to details or the method in which any one of these objects is to be attained, there is practical unanimity in the opinion that our commercial expansion must go on; that the industrial supremacy which is now conceded to us by all the world must be maintained and strengthened by every means in our power; that there can be no turning back to the position of isolation and exclusiveness which, now that we are producing more than we can consume, would inevitably mean repletion, stagnation and finally, decay. It is this feeling which has converted us from a quiet, self-centered people absorbed with our affairs, into a strenuous force among the nations—not necessarily aggressive or militant, but determined to avail ourselves to the full of our new and constantly widening opportunities, and to safeguard the novel interests which are springing up in the spread of American commerce throughout the world. . . .

It may be assumed that our continued growth on present lines depends upon the steady progress of commercial expansion. The question as to how increasing trade may best be secured and maintained is one as to which our publicists and politicians differ widely. Nearly all of them concur substantially in the view expressed by President McKinley at Buffalo, that "we must not repose in fancied security that we can forever sell everything and buy little or nothing," and that "a system which provides a mutual exchange of commodities is manifestly essential to the continued and healthful growth of our export trade"; but there are powerful interests which will antagonize many of the tariff concessions that such a policy implies. If we make no concessions we may ultimately find ourselves face to face with impassable barriers raised by European nations against our manufactured goods.

There is another danger which may be imminent. Again and again our businessmen have shown a remarkable capacity for settling knotty problems independently of legislation, and our manufacturers have recently given a significant and disturbing evidence of this faculty by seeking a short cut to tariff favors in Europe without waiting for action by Congress. According to Mr. Robert P. Porter, formerly Director of the Census and a well known writer on economic subjects, American industries are establishing plants in England in order to obtain the benefit of minimum tariff rates from European countries which, in the absence of reciprocal agreements, may continue to enforce the maximum rates against the United States, if they do not make them still higher. The same thing is being done in Germany and Belgium by some of our capitalists. Such a movement, if it became general among our exporting manufacturers, would obviously be most injurious to American labor in transferring production for export from our home factories to those established in Europe, and to our export trade generally and the many important interests it subserves. Our future expansion, therefore, seems to depend upon an early adjustment of tariff differences with other countries which will remove the incentive to our manufacturers to go abroad.

There are other serious disadvantages we might easily suffer from if nothing is done to bring about the reduction of the high customs duties which many countries now enforce against our goods, even in the absence of expressly retaliatory action by those nations which are feeling most acutely the pinch of American competition. Europe has been taking our tools, our machinery, our textiles and other goods in increasing quantities because they have been found to be better and relatively cheaper than their own, even with the tariff duty added; but European purchases from us are obviously dependent upon the ability to pay, and in periods of depression, such as that which has overtaken Germany, the consumer would be forced to economize and content himself with an inferior article at the lowest price. In that event the European manufacturer might be compelled to dispose of accumulated stocks at a sacrifice that would make competition difficult for us if we continued to be handicapped by discriminating duties.

The perils which are thus seen to confront our future expansion are neither fanciful nor speculative. At any moment they may become urgent. Great as we are, with unequalled capabilities as an exporting nation, we are not great enough to set aside the natural laws of trade and make the whole world a passive instrument of our will. "We cannot hope," said Senator Lodge, in his address before the Middlesex Club in Boston, early in November, "to shut our own markets absolutely to the world and then sell to all mankind. It might be an ideal situation, but in the long run it is impracticable as well as dangerous." "The period of exclusiveness," declared President McKinley, in what has been justly termed his political testament to the American people, "is past. The expansion of our trade and commerce is the pressing problem. Commercial wars are unprofitable. A policy of good will and friendly trade relations will prevent reprisals."

(From *World's Work*, January, 1902, III, 1614-1623)

BROOKS ADAMS, *The New Empire*, 1902

During the last decade the world has traversed one of those periodic crises which attend an alteration in the social equilibrium. The seat of energy has migrated from Europe to America. The phenomenon is not new, as similar perturbations have occurred from the earliest times; its peculiarity lies in its velocity and its proportions. A change of equilibrium has heretofore occupied at least the span of a human lifetime, so that a new generation has gradually become habituated to the novel environment. In this instance the revolution came so suddenly that few realized its presence before it ended. Nevertheless, it has long been in preparation, and it appears to be fundamental, for it is the effect of that alteration in mental processes which we call the advance of science.

American supremacy has been made possible only through applied science. The labors of successive generations of scientific men have established a control over nature which has enabled the United States to construct a new industrial mechanism, with processes surpassingly perfect. Nothing has ever equalled in economy and energy the administration of the great American corporations. These are the offspring of scientific thought. On the other hand, wherever scientific criticism and scientific methods have not penetrated the old processes prevail, and these show signs of decrepitude. The national government may be taken as an illustration.

When Englishmen first settled upon this continent they came as pioneers, and they developed an extreme individuality. Thinly scattered in widely separated colonies along the coast, little independent communities came into being which had few interests in common. Consolidation began late and took an imperfect form, the conditions then existing generating a peculiar administrative mechanism. The organization reached after the Revolution was rather negative than positive. The people suffered from certain effects of decentralization which interfered with commercial exchanges. These they tried to remedy, but they deprecated corporate energy. They provided against discriminations in trade, violations of contract, bad money, and the like, and they made provision for the common defense, but they manifested jealousy of consolidated power.

Each state feared interference in local concerns more than it craved aid in schemes which transcended its borders, and accordingly the framers of the Constitution intentionally made combined action slow and difficult. They devised three coordinate departments, each of which could stop the other two, and none of which could operate alone. And they did this under the conviction that they had reached certain final truths in government, and in the face of the law that friction bears a ratio to the weight moved.

Even with such concessions to tradition, no little energy was required to overcome the inertia of that primitive society, for on such societies tradition has a preponderating influence. Patrick Henry well represented conservative Virginia, and Henry denounced the Constitution day by day "as the most fatal plan which could possibly be conceived for enslaving a free people." Henry could not comprehend the change in the conditions of life about him, because he had been bred to believe that the institutions he knew were intrinsically good. He revered them much as he revered religion; as an end in themselves, not as means to an end. Every considerable political innovation must thus affect a portion of the population, for men always live to whom a change in what they have been trained to respect is tantamount to sacrilege. This temper of the mind is conservatism. It resists change instinctively and not intelligently, and it is this conservatism which largely causes those violent explosions of pent-up energy which we term revolutions. Still, changes, peaceful or bloody, must come, and it behooves each generation to take care that such as it shall have to deal with shall be accepted without shock. Intellectual rigidity is the chief danger, for resistance to the inevitable is proportionate to intellectual rigidity. . . .

Take economics as an example. During the eighteenth century Adam Smith, having carefully observed the conditions which prevailed in Europe and especially in Great Britain, wrote a book admirably suited to his environment. Then others theorized on these commentators, and their successors upon them, until the most practical of business problems has been lost in a metaphysical fog.

Now men are apt to lecture on political economy as if it were a dogma, much as the nominalists and realists lectured in medieval schools. But *a priori* theories can avail little in matters which are determined by experiment.

Political economy as a dogma is as absurd as would be a dogma which taught an infallible way to manipulate the stock market. Success in competition comes solely through a comprehension of existing conditions and the capacity to take advantage of opportunities. One community, such as Rome, may do well by robbery; another, like Great Britain, when she enjoyed a monopoly of minerals and of manufactures, may flourish upon free trade; a third, like Germany with her sugar policy, may find her advantage in attacking a rival by export bounties; while a fourth may thrive by seclusion, as did Japan, as long as circumstances favored. No one can say *a priori* what will succeed; the criterion is success.

The inference is that if a man would study economics to some purpose, he must study them practically, as he would any other business. He must begin by learning the principles of trade and finance as they are presented by actual daily experience, just as the soldier, the sailor, the lawyer, and the doctor learn their professions. Then if he wish to generalize, he can examine into the experience of other countries, past and present, and observe how they won or lost. In other words, he can read geography, history, archaeology, numismatics, and kindred branches, and extend his horizon at his pleasure. Thus men work who expect to earn their bread in the walks of active life, but colleges do not classify.

History, geography, and economics are related branches which mutually explain each other, and none of which can be well understood alone. They also aid each other, for the sequence of cause and effect sustains the memory; and yet they are never taught together, although to learn the three combined would take little longer, and demand less effort, than to learn any one singly. It is a curious commentary on liberal methods, that geography, which is eminently practical, is only applied in military or possibly technical schools. There is, perhaps, no thorough collection of maps made on scientific principles in any public library in the United States.

Lastly, it remains to consider how the introduction of inductive methods in social matters would affect the community at large by the destruction of its ideals; for ideals would probably suffer.

He who is dominated by tradition exalts the past. In the concrete case of an American, he believes more or less implicitly that the contemporaries of Washington and Jefferson arrived at political truths which, at least so far as he is concerned, may be received as final. The man who reasons by induction views the work of Washington and Jefferson otherwise. He views it as the product of the conditions of the eighteenth century, and as having no more necessary relation to the conduct of affairs in the twentieth, than Franklin's methods in electricity would have to the manipulation of a modern dynamo. The United States now occupies a position of extraordinary strength. Favored alike by geographical position, by deposits of minerals, by climate, and by the character of her population, she has little to fear, either in peace or war, from rivals, provided the friction created by the movement of the masses with which she has to deal does not neutralize her energy.

Masses accumulate in the United States because administration by masses is cheaper than administration by detail. Masses take the form of corporations, and the men who rise to the control of these corporations rise because they are the fittest. The process is natural selection. The life of the community lies in these masses. Derange them, and there would immediately follow an equivalent loss of energy. They are there because the conditions of our civilization are such as to make it cheaper that they should be there, and if our political institutions are ill-adapted to their propagation and development, then political institutions must be readjusted, or the probability is that the whole fabric of society will be shattered by the dislocation of the economic system. America holds its tenure of prosperity only on condition that she can undersell her rivals, and she cannot do so if her administrative machinery generates friction unduly.

Political institutions and political principles are but a conventional dial on whose face the hands revolve which mark the movement of the mechanism within. Most governments and many codes have been adored as emanating from the deity. All were ephemeral, and all which survived their purpose became a jest or a curse to the children of the worshippers; things to be cast aside like worn-out garments.

Under any circumstances an organism so gigantic as the American Union must generate friction. In American industry friction will infallibly exist between capital and labor; but that necessary friction may be indefinitely increased by conservatism. History teems with examples of civilizations which have been destroyed through an unreasoning inertia, like that of Brutus, or the French privileged classes, or Patrick Henry. A slight increase in the relative cost of production caused by an imperfect mechanical adjustment is usually sufficient to give some rival an advantage, and when a country is undersold, misery sets in. People who cannot earn their daily bread are revolutionary, and disorders bred by violence achieve the series of disasters which began with the diversion of trade. Such was the fate of the great cities of Flanders, of Bruges, of Ghent, and of Ypres.

The alternative presented is plain. Men may cherish ideals and risk substantial benefits to realize them. Such is the emotional instinct. Or they may regard their government dispassionately, as they would any other matter of business.

Americans in former generations led a simple agricultural life. Possibly such a life was a happier one than ours. Very probably keen competition is not a blessing. We cannot alter our environment. Nature has cast the United States into the vortex of the fiercest struggle which the world has ever known. She has become the heart of the economic system of the age, and she must maintain her supremacy by wit and by force, or share the fate of the discarded.

(From *The New Empire*, New York, 1902, pp. xi-xiii, xxx-xxxiv)

FRANK A. VANDERLIP, "The American 'Commercial Invasion' of Europe," 1902

The European view of the competitive positions which the great nations occupy in the struggle for international trade development is just now a matter of keen interest to the people of the United States. As an officer in the financial department of the Government, during the period of the most extraordinary development in the whole history of our foreign trade relations, I was especially interested in this subject. I wanted the point of view and the conclusions of some of the men who were equally interested observers, but who were looking at the development from without rather than from within. For four years I had seen at close range the growth of a favorable balance of trade which had assumed a total in that brief period greater than had been the net trade balance from the founding of the Government up to that time. That was a phenomenon which had had few parallels in our economic history, and the desire to study it from the European point of view led me to visit nearly all the countries of Europe. . . .

The subject I discussed with these distinguished foreigners is one regarding which our public has been pretty thoroughly enlightened in the last five years, and it is one of which the European public has heard almost as much in the English and Continental newspapers, but from quite an opposite point of view. When the amount of our sales to foreign countries passed the $1,000,000,000 mark in 1897, we began to congratulate ourselves on the strides we were making in the markets of the world. The record was followed by steadily growing totals, until now we have, in a 12-month, sent to other nations commodities to the value of $1,500,000,000. The meaning of that total is emphasized if we look back and find it compares with an average during the ten years ending 1896 of $825,000,000.

While our sales to foreign countries have grown so prodigiously, the other side of our financial account during these last five or six years has shown no proportionate increase. We have bought from the foreigners an average of only $800,000,000 a year, and that total has shown little tendency to expand. It was this fact, this mighty development of our sales, while our purchases were, comparatively, on a declining scale, which piled up in half a dozen years a favorable balance of trade so enormous as to startle the world. In the last six years we have sold in merchandise, produce, and manufactures $2,000,000,000 more than we have bought; while in all our history, from the beginning of the Government up to six years ago, the foreign trade balance in our favor had aggregated a net total of only $383,000,000.

The significance of these surprising totals was recognized on both sides of the Atlantic. An analysis of them brought out features more important than the vastness of the aggregate. Heretofore our sales had been made up almost wholly of foodstuffs and raw materials. Europe was the workshop. But that has changed, and we find, year after year, an astonishing increase in our exports of manufactured articles, an increase that in the last two or three years reached totals which gave ample basis for the popular talk of our invasion of the European industrial fields. Our exports of manufactured articles in the decade prior to 1897 averaged $163,000,000 annually. In 1898 our sales of manufactured articles to foreign customers jumped to $290,-000,000, the next year to $339,000,000, the next to $434,000,000.

These figures, showing a steady invasion by our manufacturers of foreign industrial fields, have a natural corollary. As exports of manufactures increased, our imports of the handiwork of foreign shops showed an even more rapid decline. Our manufacturers were not only invading the foreigners' own markets, meeting him at his threshold with a new competition, but they were taking away from him his greatest market—the United States. We have in the last half-dozen years been manufacturing for ourselves a vast amount of goods, such as we have been accustomed to buy abroad.

One can turn from a contemplation of these great totals to an examination of the records made in recent years by individual industries, and find in detail facts upon which to base a belief that the United States has acquired, or is acquiring, supremacy in the world's markets. So many industries have been sending rapidly increasing contributions to swell the rising tide of our foreign commerce that it is difficult to tell any detailed story of American commercial expansion without making it read like a trade catalogue. The increase in our exports of manufactured articles can, in the main, be traced to advances made in the manufacture of iron and steel, and to the display of inventive talent in the making of machinery. The development of our grasp on the world's market for articles manufactured from iron and steel has been no surprise to those who early recognized the position of America in respect to the raw materials from which those articles are produced. America unquestionably possesses advantages, in respect to her iron ore and her coal mines, far superior to those of any other country, and, based solidly upon that superiority, has already become the greatest producer of iron and steel in the world.

American locomotives, running on American rails, now whistle past the Pyramids and across the long Siberian steppes. They carry the Hindoo pilgrims from all parts of their empire to the sacred waters of the Ganges. Three years ago there was but one American locomotive in the United Kingdom; to-day there is not a road of importance there on which trains are not being pulled by American engines. The American locomotive has successfully invaded France. The Manchurian Railway, which is the real beginning of oriental railway-building, bought all its rails and rolling-stock in the United States. American bridges span rivers on every continent. American cranes are swinging over many foreign moles. Wherever there are extensive harvests there may be found American machinery to gather the grain. In every great market of the world tools can have no better recommendation than the mark "Made in America.". . .

That the United States gives promises of reaching a position of industrial supremacy in the world's trade is acknowledged to-day the world over. Undoubtedly we have been too flamboyant in some of our claims. The industrial world as yet is by no means prostrate at our feet. We have before us a long campaign of hard work and intelligent prosecution of every advantage which we have, before we reach such a position of industrial supremacy as occasional newspaper writers on both sides of the Atlantic have given us credit for. That we have the foundation upon which to build such industrial supremacy, however, cannot be doubted by any one who is familiar with the resources and abilities shown in our own industrial field, and makes intelligent comparison with the conditions that obtain abroad.

It ought to be kept in mind that the road to the commercial domination of the world is not a clear one for us, and that as yet we are a long way from the end of it. Evidences of that will be found in studying current statistics of our manufactured exports. The rapid increase which has been going on for a number of years has halted, and for the last fiscal year reports show a decrease. That decrease can be accounted for by the fact that our shipments to Porto Rico, Hawaii, and the Philippines are no longer counted foreign exports, but it is, nevertheless, evident that a halt has come in the triumphant march of American manufactures toward European markets. An important reason for this is in the very force of the success we have made. There have been serious inroads made in the prosperity of many foreign manufactures by our successful competition. The depression has been reflected in lower wages and in decreased purchasing power, and a lower level of prices which has reacted on us in common with the foreign manufacturers.

In a good many directions we have much to learn in regard to a successful prosecution of foreign trade. The Germans could give us valuable lessons. They are strong in two particulars—strong in the line of technical education, though perhaps not superior to us, and strong in commercial training specially adapted to the needs of their representatives in foreign countries. In this last particular we are lamentably weak. We do not learn languages readily, and we have been too busy with our home affairs to cultivate what facility we have. It is a comparatively difficult thing to find trained businessmen, born in America, who speak fluently two or more Continental languages, and it follows from that difficulty that we send commercial representatives to Europe who are under the almost hopeless handicap of not speaking the language of a country in which they wish to do business. Were it not for the coming universality of the English language, the handicap would be far greater than it is. Unfortunately the bad equipment of many of the commercial representatives who are sent abroad is not confined to their lack of knowledge of languages. Frequently they have but vague ideas of the commercial geography of Europe. They are not at all clear as to what particular sections are given over to this form of manufacturing or that field of production. More than half the failures that have come to manufacturers who have tried to extend their foreign business have resulted from the lack of qualifications in the representatives they sent abroad.

Another condition that is not favorable to our development is one that is being thought of a good deal more in Europe than at home. We no longer are occupying the leading position in scientific investigation having special commercial application. Many of the most notable discoveries of the last few years in commercial chemistry, electricity, and other fields of scientific work having direct relation with industry have been made by foreigners. The X-ray and the wireless telegraph are illustrations which would occur to every one, but there have been numberless important discoveries of great value in industrial operations for which we are obliged to pay royalty to foreign inventors. . . .

The most important of all obstacles that the development of our foreign trade is likely to encounter is the same one which has proved the most dangerous rock in the path of English industry—the growth of a spirit in trades-unions which attempts to regulate the business of employers in other matters than those relating to wages and hours of labor. I believe the decline of English industry can be attributed to the success of labor organizations in restricting the amount of work a man may be permitted to do, more than to any other single cause. We have encountered that spirit too frequently in our own labor field, and it is one which, if successfully persisted in, will cut the ground of advantage from under our manufacturers quicker than anything else I know of. . . .

But in Germany we find not only a state with apparently a great future, but a state which has begun to realize that future in a thoroughly modern way. The system of education, elementary, secondary, and university, certainly rivals our own, and is probably superior to it. It is a system which leaves less than three per cent of the population illiterate, and sifts out the brightest minds and trains them for the service of the State. The State in turn is eager and anxious to avail itself of the services of men who have won intellectual distinction. There is a system of commercial education whose founders realized that successfully to deal with foreigners requires a speaking and writing knowledge of their language. There is a national and municipal administration which in their effectiveness and absolute integrity must bring shame to the resident of almost any American city when he compares them with conditions surrounding him at home. The Government has encouraged commerce and foreign trade with great intelligence. It has established the gold standard and so organized the Reichsbank, that the mechanism of exchange has the foundation of secure confidence. It has aided in the establishment of German banks abroad, and placed German traders in the position of distinct advantage in pushing their commercial conquests. A trained consular service has been developed, composed of men who speak the language of the country to which they are sent and who use the language to find out whatever may be of service to the German exporter.

The Government has pursued a consistent policy in its trade relations and commercial treaties, which has all along been wisely adapted to the needs of the national economy. While the industries were getting a foothold, they were protected by high duties. When their development had reached the stage of independence, and when their chief need was new markets, the Government made concessions to neighboring States in the customs tariff, and, by a series of treaties completed in 1893, admitted raw materials at low duties in return for similar privileges conceded to German manufactured exports. The Government early saw that private railway management in Germany was unfavorable to the export trade, because it had not learned the lesson of scientific rate-making, which we in the United States have only in recent years mastered. Perceiving this fact, the German Government took most of the private lines, and added to them until, in 1901, out of 30,777 miles of railway more than 27,000 belonged to the State. In full control of the railway system, the State administration has worked out, very successfully, the basic principles of rate-making, to increase the rates with the value of the freight. It has granted low rates on iron and coal, to which concessions the iron and steel industry of Westphalia owes in large measure its prosperity. The German Government also has not hesitated to use the bounty system to build up the national industries. The beet-sugar industry owes its existence quite as much to the aid of the State as to the painstaking care of the owner and scientist, and in a single year the exports of sugar and glucose to Great Britain from Germany have amounted to more than $50,000,000. The German merchant marine has been intelligently assisted by liberal subsidies. I found among business men a quite general agreement as to the great benefits which industry and commerce had derived from subsidies.

(From *Scribner's Magazine,* January–March, 1902, XXXI, 3-22, 194-213, 287-306)

FRED MACKENZIE, "The Invaders," 1901

In the domestic life we have got to this: The average man rises in the morning from his New England sheets, he shaves with "Williams" soap and a Yankee safety razor, pulls on his Boston boots over his socks from North Carolina, fastens his Connecticut braces, slips his Waltham or Waterbury watch in his pocket, and sits down to breakfast. There he congratulates his wife on the way her Illinois straight-front corset sets off her Massachusetts blouse, and he tackles his breakfast, where he eats bread made from prairie flour (possibly doctored at the special establishments on the lakes), tinned oysters from Baltimore and a little Kansas City bacon, while his wife plays with a slice of Chicago ox-tongue. The children are given "Quaker" oats. At the same time he reads his morning paper printed by American machines, on American paper, with American ink, and, possibly edited by a smart journalist from New York City.

He rushes out, catches the electric tram (New York) to Shepard's Bush, where he gets in a Yankee elevator to take him on to the American-fitted electric railway to the City.

At his office, of course, everything is American. He sits on a Nebraska swivel chair, before a Michigan roll-top desk, writes his letters on a Syracuse typewriter, signing them with a blotting-sheet from New England. The letter copies are put away in files manufactured in Grand Rapids.

At lunch-time he hastily swallows some cold roast beef that comes from the Mid-Western cow, and flavors it with Pittsburg pickles, followed by a few Delaware tinned peaches, and then soothes his mind with a couple of Virginia cigarettes.

To follow his course all day would be wearisome. But when evening comes he seeks relaxation at the latest American musical comedy, drinks a cocktail or some California wine, and finishes up with a couple of "little liver pills" made in America.

(From William T. Stead, *The Americanization of the World*, London, 1901, pp. 354-356)

RAY STANNARD BAKER, "The American Commercial Invasion of the World," 1901

More than ordinary significance attaches to the fact that in the same year, 1898, in which the United States appeared, somewhat against her will, as a great military and colonizing power, she also attained supremacy among the nations as the greatest of the world's exporters of home products. Both achievements represented victories over European nations, and the struggle with England for trade supremacy was hardly less stern than the shorter and fiercer war with Spain, and its effects may reach further into history. For more than a hundred years the United States had been absorbed in developing her own great country, in working out a new form of government, in assimilating a hundred difficult and diverse elements of population. She had been taken up with her own affairs, to the exclusion of everything else, a mere object of wonder and curiosity to Europe, not seriously accepted as a great power, roused only when some foreigner sought to meddle with her personal affairs or with those of her immediate neighbors. The attitude of the foreigner was that of a grown man toward a big, raw boy unconscious yet of his own strength. But in 1898, after years of strenuous training and self-development, the boy suddenly reached his majority. The nation was ready for its world work and its world responsibilities. No Monroe doctrine could longer wall it in, nor tariffs and wide oceans keep it out.

Every one will recall the wave of mingled astonishment, respect, and alarm which swept over Europe after the battles of Manila and Santiago. Before it had well subsided Europe heard that the United States had built a military bridge in Egypt because her iron-masters could do it more quickly and more cheaply than their English cousins, albeit they were 3,000 miles farther away. Then came the further news that American steel rails were being laid on the Trans-Siberian Railroad in northeastern China, that American locomotives were drawing trains out of London through the ancient home of the steel industry, that American flour was being sold in Finland at the very front door of Russia, with its vast wheat-fields, that American cotton cloth was driving the English product out of China, that after long opposition English manufacturers were being forced to adopt American-made tools and machines, and, more than anything else, that all the great nations of Europe were paying every year large sums of money to cancel the credit balance in favor of the United States. Trade journals, the newspapers, and the heavy reviews all over Europe began publishing articles on "United States Competition," "Why England Feels American Competition," and so on. In Germany the invasion of American products became so extended that a great political party must needs obstruct their entrance with difficult inspection regulations or force legislation to bar them out entirely, and more lately we have heard of trade combinations in Europe to fight American goods.

Indeed, the whole world seems to have awakened to the fact since 1898 that the United States has suddenly become a power to be reckoned with. The effects of the American commercial invasion are being felt sharply in every quarter. As an example, we find Mr. W. H. D. Haggard, British minister at Caracas, Venezuela, explaining to his home government why exports from the United States to Venezuela had fallen off in 1898 only 10 per cent., while British exports fell off 25 per cent.

"The question of American competition," he writes, "will, I imagine, be more serious in the future. American manufacturers have hitherto found a sufficient market in the United States. It is only lately that they have seen their production larger than their local demand, and that they have consequently begun to export in any large quantities. It is to be expected that the impetus given by the result of the war, and the consequent realization of the fact of the existence of other markets besides the United States, will increase this effect."

Consider also South Africa, an English and foreign commercial stronghold, farther by thousands of miles from the United States than from Europe: The *British South-African Gazette* prints a table showing that American exports which competed with British exports increased in the five years from 1893 to 1898 by over 139 per cent., while the non-competing exports increased 565 per cent.—a hundred per cent. a year.

We find such an authority as the London *Engineer* sorrowfully commenting on the statement that "the American engine is a more satisfactory machine than its beautifully finished English or Scotch-made brother."

"We have the best interest of the locomotive-builders of this country at heart," says the *Engineer*; "and we should wholly fail in our duty if we said pleasant things and maintained that the typical English locomotive must be the best for Austria, or South Africa, or China, or Africa, just because it is the best for the railways of the United Kingdom. We repeat that Americans more fully understand what is wanted for railway service in a new and cheap country than we do, and that we ought not to be too proud to learn from them."

The present American invasion is not confined to any one country, but reaches to every part of the earth, civilized and savage, and to almost every branch of industry. To some countries the exports are still small, but it must be remembered that the invasion has only just begun, having had its greatest activity only in the last three years, 1898, 1899, and 1900, so that it is a departure quite as new as our appearance as a colonizer. The totals of American export trade will show how recent and enormous this advance has been. In 1895, for instance, we sold abroad a little over $807,000,000 worth of our products; in 1900 we sold $1,394,000,000 worth, a gain in five years of over $587,000,000—more than the entire export business of Russia, and half that of Germany and France. And while our exports were making such strides upward our imports have increased by a comparatively small percentage—from $731,000,000 in 1895 to $850,-000,000 in 1899, a gain in five years of only $119,000,000, showing that we not only send more goods abroad, but that we more nearly supply our population at home, although it is increasing rapidly. But the total of exports does not begin to tell the story of our invasion of foreign trade markets. For many years a vast proportion of the goods sold by the United States was raw materials—such as wheat, cotton, coal, corn, live animals, and so on, and we might have kept on shipping such products in vast quantities for years without becoming a great commercial nation. But it was in the sale of manufactured goods that the nation found its most remarkable recent development. These are the goods—the bicycles, the boots and shoes, the cotton cloth, the locomotives—which have made the American invasion so dreaded by foreign nations. Every year previous to 1898—the year that the nation came to its own, and for the first time exceeded Great Britain in the vast totals of our exportation of home products—we bought more manufactured goods than we sold, but in 1898 we sold nearly $291,-000,000 worth and bought only $231,000,000 worth. In 1900 the difference was still greater: we sold $432,000,000 worth and bought only $329,000,000 worth.

Here is the summary: Of manufactured articles, in 1890 we bought $357,000,000 worth and sold $151,000,000 worth; in 1900 we bought $329,000,000 worth and sold $432,000,000—loss in ten years' imports, $28,000,000; gain in ten years' exports, $281,000,000.

This shows graphically how the volume of imports of manufactured goods has lost $28,000,000 since 1890, whereas the volume of exported articles has gained $281,000,000. This is the story in great totals of the conquest. In its particulars it is not less wonderful.

We find, for instance, that the whole world has suddenly discovered the excellence and cheapness of American boots and shoes. The old cobbler is giving way before the machinery of Yankee ingenuity. In 1889 the value of our boots and shoes sold in foreign lands was about $586,000; in 1899 the value was over $2,711,000, a fivefold increase in ten years. Paper products show equally as good a record, jumping from a little over $1,000,000 worth in 1889 to over $5,000,000 worth exported in 1899. And then, think of selling abroad over $121,000,-000 worth of a single class of products in one year! That was the record of iron and steel products in 1900, and when one pauses and thinks what enormous numbers of locomotives, pumps, printing-presses, typewriters, bicycles, sewing-machines, what quantities of farm and other machinery, steel rails, steel beams for bridges and steel plates for ships, fire-arms, stoves, wire, nails, and other products, it must take to make $121,000,000 worth, some conception may be formed perhaps of the wide distribution of American goods in foreign countries. The years 1898, 1899, and 1900 were the most prosperous in the history of this industry, the annual exports jumping from about $57,000,000 in 1897 to over $121,000,000 in 1900. The exports were large as far back as 1890, amounting to over $25,000,000 worth in that year, but since then they have nearly quintupled. Indeed, it was only seven years ago that we were actually buying more of our iron and steel products abroad than we were exporting; now we are putting our machinery even in English shops, and our locomotives on English, Indian, French, Algerian, Russian, Chinese, South African, and Egyptian roads, and selling them cheaper and delivering them more promptly than any of the foreign iron-masters are able to do.

In the matter of our exports of beef and beef products—a most important phase of American business in foreign lands—one of the largest packing-house companies in the United States says in a recent report:

"We have placed our goods in every civilized country on the globe. Europe, Asia, and Africa have been familiar with our brands for years. Upon all expeditions for discovery, including those of Nansen and Wellman in the arctic regions, our goods have been taken. Our canned meats, dried sausages, barrelled pork and beef, and smoked meats have been preferred for India, South Africa, and the distant countries of the world."

The London *Financial News,* commenting on this remarkable American foreign business in 1899, says:

"Practically, then, the United States export trade has now about an equal aggregate value with our own, while the more valuable home market is, in her case, roughly, twice as large as ours. The significance of this comparison is heightened by recollection of the circumstances that—taking a series of years and a per head basis—our export trade is, despite the recent spurt, marked by retrogression rather than progress, and that our rival represents prodigious growth—a growth showing no signs of diminution.

"The big American increase—and it may be regarded as the central fact in the situation—has been in manufactures. It can hardly be necessary to tell our readers with what special force American development in this direction strikes at England, or to discourse to them on the comparative value of an export trade in manufactures over one in raw materials and primary articles of merchandise; but it is important that they should bear these facts in mind, to illuminate their reading of the continued expansion of the exports from the United States of articles other than the four staples—breadstuffs, raw cotton, provisions, and petroleum."

And then there is China. Up to 1899 we did not take enough interest in that great empire of sleeping potentialities even to encourage our traders, while all Europe was scrambling for Chinese territory and Chinese markets. In 1899, however, we secured an "open door," but not until the trade conquest was well under way. The annual report of the inspector-general of customs of China, covering the year 1898, shows an increase of nearly 40 per cent. in imports into China from the United States, while the increase in total imports from all countries is less than 5 per cent. Imports into China from the United States in 1898 were over 17,000,000 Jaikwan taels, against 12,000,000 taels in 1897, an increase of 4,000,000 taels, while those from Great Britain, our most active rival in Oriental trade, fell from 40,000,000 taels in 1897 to nearly 35,000,000 taels in 1898, and from the continent of Europe the 1898 imports also showed a slight reduction, being 10,000,-000 taels against 11,000,000 taels.

The sale of American cotton goods in China will indicate how our invasion is progressing. American sheetings entered at Shanghai increased from 380,000 pieces in the three months ended September 30, 1895, to over 1,000,000 pieces in the same period in 1899, whereas English sheetings increased only from 101,000 pieces to 224,000 pieces, and Indian sheetings decreased from 30,000 pieces to a bare 5,000 pieces. A still more remarkable record was made for American drills and jeans.

A showing almost equally impressive is made by our next-door neighbor, Canada, a loyal British possession. In order to favor English goods especially the Canadian government gave them 25 per cent. preference in the tariffs, but in spite of all this, American exports have been increasing actually more rapidly than English exports. Indeed, Canada bought nearly $2,000,000 less of English goods in the fiscal year 1899 than she did in 1894, while she bought over $36,000,000 worth more from the United States. She is willing to sell to Great Britain and she has immense quantities of products to sell, but she prefers to buy of the United States.

Of all the continents, South America shows the least effects of the American invasion. While our exports to our southern neighbors increased materially in 1898, 1899, and 1900, the percentages are not as large as in Asia, Oceanica, Europe, or Africa, or on our own continent. This is due mostly to unsatisfactory transportation facilities; we are hampered by lack of ships. Moreover, Germany has made some of her greatest trade successes in South America, and she will undoubtedly be our bitterest commercial enemy there for years to come.

Possibly the most remarkable and important feature, in more ways than one, of America's commercial invasion, is in the business and the business possibilities of our new possessions, the Philippines, Porto Rico, Hawaii, and of Cuba. Although we have barely assumed control of these islands, the total exports from the United States to the islands amounted in the fiscal year 1900 to considerably more than $47,000,-000, as compared with about $17,000,000 in 1898—a gain of $30,-000,000 in two years. Considering the fact that neither Cuba nor Porto Rico has yet returned to anything like normal conditions, and that there was a condition of actual warfare in the Philippines during all of 1899 and 1900, the fact that the total exports to the islands in those years exceed those of the palmiest days of reciprocity, indicates a bright future for our commercial invasion of those islands.

It is estimated that in ordinary times the new islands will consume $100,000,000 worth of foreign goods annually, and export about $125,-000,000 worth. In 1900 the United States exported $47,000,000, or nearly one-half of the total requirements, and imported about $61,000,-000, more than three-fifths of the requirements. Under an honest administration and with proper development the islands can be made to produce much more extensively, and therefore to buy more freely. So that the promise of a big future business in the islands is most excellent. Besides this, the manufacture of goods especially adapted to these tropical climes will place the United States in a position to compete much more readily with other tropical countries, a fact upon which more than one British consul has already spoken a warning. . . :

The average American is a great traveller. He knows more about England, France, and Germany and their needs than they know about him and his needs. Never before, indeed, was there such a rush of Americans to Europe as in 1899 and 1900. The number of cabin passengers at the port of New York in 1899 alone reached over 107,-000, compared with 80,000 in 1898. The steerage passengers numbered nearly 304,000, compared with about 220,000 in 1898, showing what an army of Americans have a familiar knowledge of Europe. In the same way the last two years has seen many more Americans travelling to the Orient, to South America, to Cuba, to the Philippines, than ever before, learning the customs and language and needs of these people. The little matter of passports issued by the State Department in Washington will show this tendency admirably. In January, 1900, no fewer than 1500 passports were issued against only 680 in the corresponding month in 1898.

American newspapers are full of London, Paris, and Berlin despatches, whereas it must be an American event of extraordinary importance to make a prominent showing in a European paper. For years the principal American news in London papers was the news of lynchings, crimes, and Indian raids.

Another factor which has contributed to American success is the position of the United States, fronting as it does on two oceans, and nearer by many days' travel to the great markets of the Orient than Europe. Moreover, the country is closely knit together with railroads and telegraphs, and freight rates are remarkably low. For instance, a bushel of wheat or an equivalent amount of flour can be shipped from Minneapolis to almost any point in western Europe for about 20 cents. This includes no fewer than three reshipments—at Duluth, Buffalo, and New York. It costs almost as much to ship the same wheat from Liverpool to Manchester in England. Moreover, railroad and steamship communication is growing more extended every year. In 1899 more than 4,557 miles of new railroad were built, the greatest record since 1892. This excellent interior communication has lent to the development of other great shipping ports besides New York, so that the foreign conquest can go forward from many parts of the country. New Orleans, Boston, Baltimore, Galveston, Newport News, Tacoma, Seattle, have been creeping up in comparison with New York, their prosperity during the past two years being greater than ever before.

The only disagreeable feature about the American invasion is that it is being made largely in foreign ships. The United States has a magnificent fleet of coastwise and lake vessels, but the freights on its colossal foreign business go largely into the pockets of foreign ship-owners. While we equal England in our exports and far exceed any other nation, we have only about one-fourteenth of the tonnage engaged in foreign business. Germany, France, and Norway are well ahead of us. Although millions of dollars' worth of American goods go through the Suez Canal, the American flag is not seen there on a merchant vessel more than three or four times in a year. Moreover, the American shipping business is increasing little or none. It has actually decreased since 1860, and the increase since 1890 has been only 325,000 tons, whereas the merchant navies of almost every other nation in the world have increased very largely. Great Britain jumped from 4,000,000 tons in 1840, at a time when America was nearly as great on the seas as the mother-country, to nearly 14,000,000 tons in 1898. In the same time little Norway jumped from less than 300,000 tons to nearly 1,700,000 tons.

Remarkable as has been the growth of American foreign business in the last two years, the commercial conquest is only just beginning. Great opportunities and possibilities bring with them great responsibilities. The American businessman, if he would continue to win victories, must needs have plain honesty and the shrewd foresight which will prevent him from abusing his power. Only a few years ago the United States sold thousands of tons of cheese abroad. In some years two-thirds of our entire cheese product went to England. The profits were good and the business was growing, but one day the greed of the exporter got the better of him. He thought his foreign customer wouldn't know the difference, and so he sent out filled, adulterated, and counterfeit cheeses. Almost before he knew it our European cheese-market was absolutely ruined. If the conquest, therefore, is to go on, the American must exercise the honesty that will make the name "United States" on an article the sure sign of its perfection, and the vigilance that meets instantly the price and excellence of every competing product.

(From *Harper's Weekly*, February 16, 1901, XLV, 174-175)

ROBERT P. PORTER, "Our European Trade," 1900

Not so very long ago, when I used to discuss tariff questions with the late Judge Kelley, of Pennsylvania, and with that Democratic protectionist from the same State, the Hon. Samuel J. Randall, the idea was to secure protection for our metal schedule, so that we could manufacture at home the 100 million dollars' worth of manufactures of iron and steel which we once purchased abroad. We must make our own steel rails, our own tin plate, our own nails, our own pipes, our own steel wire, they argued in those days, and in doing so give employment to American labor. I recall preparing for Mr. Randall— before the debate on the proposed Morrison Bill, reducing duties horizontally—a little table, showing how much of these and kindred commodities we at that time were buying abroad. I demonstrated to Mr. Randall that we could just as well make all these things at home, and thereby employ 200,000 additional laborers. Mr. Randall was not a man you could load down with a bushel basket of statistics. He was concise and to the point, and the little table in question only made one sheet of note-paper. I gave it to him in his committee room at the House of Representatives. He was busy, but he read it over two or three times and put it into his pocket. That night he sent for me to come to his house. I went there, and he said: "Porter, if these figures are reliable—and they seem to be within the mark—I will never vote for the Morrison Bill, nor for any other bill that will cut duties on iron and steel, cotton goods, woollens, leather, chemicals, etc., until we have our home market secure." I satisfied Mr. Randall of the reliability of my estimates, and history tells what he did with the Morrison Bill. That both Judge Kelley and Mr. Randall, and later, Major, now President, McKinley, builded better than they knew, we all must now admit. The voice of the old-time free-trader seems hushed in the presence of the marvellous changes that have taken place since Kelley and Randall and McKinley fought for the home market for American labor. If we could have injected some of the following facts into those debates as prophecies, how the free-trade leaders would have sizzled! For example, the exports of iron and steel and their manufactures increased from $21,156,077 in 1889 to $93,715,951 in 1899, or nearly $72,560,000. I tabulate some of the items of these and other exports, and it will be seen they cover a wide range of manufactures:

	1889.	1899.
Steel rails	$ 235,377	$ 5,298,125
Sewing machines	2,247,875	3,264,344
Typewriting machines	No reports.	2,449,205
Shoe machinery	" "	853,936
Locomotive engines	1,227,149	4,728,748
Electrical and unspecified machinery	1,924,380	1,507,610
Builders' hardware	1,700,390	7,842,372
Nails and spikes	448,146	1,864,596
Pipes and fittings	No reports.	5,874,228
Steel wire	594,616	3,891,180
Agricultural implements	3,623,769	12,432,197
Carriages, etc.	3,090,521	9,860,164
Chemicals, drugs and dyes	5,542,753	10,995,289
Cotton manufactures	10,212,644	23,567,914
Leather and manufactures	10,747,716	23,466,985
Wool and manufactures	26,910,672	41,679,416

Above are included only a few of the items which, as I recall it, composed the memorandum I prepared for Mr. Randall. We are not only supplying the bulk of the home market, but we are exporting, in large and increasing quantities, the very class of goods which 15 years ago we were purchasing abroad. Surely on this point *The Sun,* of New York, was justified in saying last August:

> The enormous increase in the exports of American manufactures during the last ten years, and more particularly during the last two years, affords a suggestion which must be heeded by all sensible and practical men—that our economic policy is working satisfactorily. So strong has this evidence appeared to Mr. William R. Grace, an old-time "revenue reformer" of the Cleveland school, for instance, that he now frankly announces that he is convinced of the practical error of his past theory. Under our policy of protection we have built up manufacturing industries which are now successfully competing in the markets of the world with

those of foreign nations, besides supplying a constantly increasing proportion of our domestic demand.

Verily, such figures must stagger even old-time revenue reformers. Now that our foreign commerce has reached nearly $2,000,000,000, we can well afford to give it serious attention. It will not drift along as heretofore. Russia, while exceedingly partial to the United States in purchasing railway equipment and supplies, and machinery of all sorts which she is not prepared to make in sufficient quantities herself, is, at the same time, energetically looking after the European markets for the products of her strongest industries. Her treaty with Germany, her friendly relations with France and her recent overtures to England are all in the line of a policy which has for its basic principle the broadening of the European markets for Russian foodstuffs, petroleum oil, mineral products, wool, timber, fibres, hides and skins. The activities of Russia, which we admire so much and on which so much has lately been written, mean a necessity for greater activities on our part to retain the markets for our exports of agricultural products and of raw material, which, as I have pointed out, have not declined with the stupendous increase in our exports of manufactures. As our home market becomes less attractive to the European manufacturer he will naturally become less friendly to the United States and more willing to encourage his own Government to make commercial alliance with the great European Power which is doing so much to bring the Far East, with all its possibilities, nearer Continental Europe. Those American concerns which compete with commodities supplied also by Russia will testify to the great activity of Russian commercial interests at the present time, not only in every country of Continental Europe, but in England. Russia, for example, was able to secure a treaty with Germany, in spite of the violent opposition of the Agrarian party, which makes it impossible for Germany to increase the duty on Russian corn while the treaty lasts. This treaty also gave Russia other decided advantages in the importation of products, some of which compete with American products. While the German Government itself has been inclined to deal fairly with the United States, there is a very considerable element in the body politic of that country that would not hesitate to discriminate against American products, by refusing, on one pretence or another, to recognize the "most favored nation" clause—a clause which some say exists in our various treaties with the several German States, though others claim that it is absent from these treaties. For the moment, as we have seen, our trade relations with Great Britain seem to be in a satisfactory condition, while the signing of the Commercial Treaty with France places our trade with the great European Republic in a more favorable state than it has been in for many years. The most favored nation clause given us in that treaty on some special articles, together with the minimum rates on others, will keep our French trade, so long as the treaty is in force, on a satisfactory basis. The treaty will be of decided advantage, and will prevent the anxieties which have constantly arisen in the minds of American merchants, who did not know what changes might be made from time to time in the rates. These changes—that is, from minimum to maximum—it was within the power of the Ministry to make without asking for legislation, and much of our trade depended upon "ministerial courtesy," brought about by the activity and popularity of the American Ambassador at Paris. Those not within the inner circle of diplomacy can have no conception of the constant calls upon our Ambassador to plead with his French ministerial colleagues not to disturb these rates, which were liable to fluctuate with the political barometer. For example, a sudden outburst of friendship for Russia might end in granting her the minimum rates, while articles of similar character from the United States remained at the maximum until "ministerial courtesy" brought them down. However, this is, I hope, ended now.

Our trade and commercial relations with Germany are of even greater importance than those with France; for, next to the United Kingdom, our business with the Fatherland is of greater magnitude than with any other nation. In the early part of last year, when I spent six weeks in Berlin studying our trade relations with Germany, considerable anxiety was experienced by German officials as to the future of that trade, some going so far as to claim that it was getting altogether one-sided. I did not at that time think the claim reasonable, though the figures for 1898 showed a large balance of trade in favor of the United States and against Germany. Several natural causes contributed to this result. In the first place, we had purchased an unusually small amount of sugar in 1898, because, the year preceding, we had purchased an unusually large quantity. A fact which none of our Berlin critics realized was that our imports of sugar during 1898 were the smallest in 12 years, amounting to only 2,690,000,000 pounds. Compared with the record-breaking returns for 1897, when our imports reached the high figures of 4,919,000,000 pounds, these figures show a falling off of about 2,229,000,000 pounds. From a sugar bill of nearly $100,000,000, we dropped with a thud to a sugar bill of $60,000,-000. Germany, in common with other sugar-producing countries, shared the loss. Having the previous year enjoyed this prosperity, the complaint was unreasonable and only indulged in by the Agrarian organs. The following table shows the imports from and exports to Germany from 1889 to 1899:

	Imports from Germany into United States.	Exports to Germany from United States.
1889	$ 81,742,546	$ 68,002,594
1890	98,837,683	85,563,312
1891	97,316,383	92,795,456
1892	82,907,553	105,521,558
1893	96,210,203	83,578,988
1894	69,387,905	92,357,163
1895	81,014,065	92,053,753
1896	94,240,833	97,897,197
1897	111,210,614	125,246,088
1898	69,697,378	155,039,972
1899	84,242,745	155,772,279

Here we have a view of our German trade for 11 years. It will be noted that, while the exports to Germany remain practically the same in 1899 as in 1898, the imports from Germany into the United States have increased, roughly speaking, about $15,000,000. This should encourage our German friends. Long before the figures were published I told them we should import more goods from Germany this year, but they said that was only a forecast and could cut no figure in the serious facts which were facing them. We imported $8,000,000 worth more sugar this fiscal year than last, with the strong probability that the calendar year will make a better showing. The balance of trade in favor of the United States in the fiscal year 1899 was $71,529,476, against $85,342,594 in 1898, $14,035,474 in 1897 and $3,656,364 in 1896. During the decade 1890-1899 there have been seven occasions on which the balance of trade was favorable to the United States, and three in which the balance was against us. The total imports into the United States from Germany in the decade 1890-1899 were $885,-065,402, and the total exports from the United States to Germany $1,085,826,756, the balance of trade in favor of the United States in the full decade being $200,761,354. This total of 800,000,000 marks is really not a serious matter to the Germans, when we consider the commodities imported. The balance of trade against England is twice this amount, or exceeding $400,000,000 every year. England, however, is in no way disturbed. Why? Because England has learned that three-quarters of all these imports means cheap food for her factory operatives, raw material for her mills, and commodities transported in British ships to be reshipped to other countries. In fact, this balance represents a source of wealth, not a loss, as the Agrarian statesman of Germany assumes. Cut off from Germany, the supply of American cotton, of mineral oils, of fertilizers, of tobacco, of copper, of lumber, of builders' materials, of turpentine, of heavy machinery, and German industries would suffer. Reduce the supply of cheap breadstuffs, lard, bacon and meats, and the people must eat more horse-flesh and black bread, paying just as much for the inferior nourishment. Three-quarters of this so-called "balance against Germany" is a balance in favor of German industries, and simply indicates that Germany is fulfilling her mission as a great industrial nation. It represents the basis of her wealth, and is in no sense a sign of decadence. A considerable portion of this "adverse balance" is altogether fictitious, and merely indicates the great prosperity of the German shipping interests of Hamburg, Bremen and other minor ports. Quantities of these goods find their way via German ports and German railways to Russia, Belgium, Austria-Hungary and other European countries—a source of wealth to the German Empire rather than of discouragement.

The statesmanship which would seek to destroy these conditions is antiquated and not, I am happy to say, in harmony with the broader policy mapped out by Caprivi and approved by the Emperor. In the seven treaties already made, the idea was to assist the development of commerce. Let us hope our own Government will be able to negotiate a treaty along similar lines, and stop the commercial friction which every now and then breaks out, threatening to upset our relations with our second most important trading nation. The main object of this treaty should be similar to the main objects of the other treaties, to secure for Germany cheaply, as imports, the necessaries of life and of the raw materials for industries, in return for which Germany might secure certain reciprocal reductions in duty on her exported industrial products. It may be urged that the reciprocal clause of the Dingley Tariff Law, giving the President the power to reduce the duty 20 per cent. on products entering the United States, has expired. The next Congress, being Republican, would undoubtedly extend this power for 12 months. If this were done, and a little more energy put into our negotiations, we could tie up a considerable amount of our foreign trade for several years to come. This should be done, and now is the time to do it. It should be borne in mind that, when our commercial relations with Great Britain, Germany and France are satisfactory, four-fifths of our European trade is covered, for, roughly speaking, of the $1,250,000,000 representing our total European trade not over $250,-000,000, or one-fifth, remains to be distributed among the minor European countries.

(From *The North American Review*, April, 1900, CLXX, 528-537)

JOHN A. KASSON, "Impressions of President McKinley," 1901

In all questions not involving points of national right and honor, all questions involving inquiries into fact and law, [President McKinley] was inclined to follow the advice of his responsible councilors who were charged with the respective departments of administration rather than to make his own personal decisions. In all that directly affected the interests of his great constituency he was peculiarly cautious and conservative. Perhaps his action in respect to the policy of treaties of reciprocity best illustrates his conservative methods of procedure, what I may call his Fabian statesmanship.

When he appointed his special plenipotentiary in charge of this work, in the autumn of 1897, he did it, apparently, only in the performance of a duty required by the Dingley Tariff Act, which had just been adopted. The attention of foreign governments was attracted to it very slowly. They were more occupied with their resentments over the great increase of the American tariff duties effected by the act than with the plan of relief also provided by the law. Many months were occupied with the preliminary studies and correspondence.

Later the Spanish War and its sequences intervened, and engaged all the attention of the President. His message of December, 1897, announced his appointment of a plenipotentiary to execute the reciprocity provisions of the law. He added only these sentences: "The negotiations are now proceeding with several governments, both European and American. It is believed that by a careful exercise of the powers conferred by that act some grievances of our own and of other countries may be either removed or largely alleviated, and that the volume of our commercial exchanges may be enlarged, with advantage to both contracting parties. Most desirable from any standpoint of national interest and patriotism is the effort to extend our foreign commerce."

In his message of 1898 he announced the reciprocal arrangement made with France under the third section of the Act, and added: "It has relieved a portion of our export trade from serious embarrassment. Further negotiations are now pending under Section 4 of the same act, with a view to the increase of trade between the two countries to their mutual advantage. Negotiations with other governments, in part interrupted by the war with Spain, are in progress under both sections of the Tariff Act. I hope to be able to announce some of the results of these negotiations during the present session of Congress."

In his message of 1899 he informed Congress of the signature of commercial conventions with France, Argentina, British Guiana, Barbados, Bermuda, Jamaica, Nicaragua, and Turks and Caicos islands; and in view of the expiration of the two years provided by the act for the performance of the work under the fourth section, he showed his increasing confidence in the utility of reciprocity treaties by announcing the future policy of the government in the following words: "Acting under the constitutional power of the Executive in respect to treaties, I have deemed it my duty, while observing the limitations of concession provided by the fourth section, to bring to a conclusion all pending negotiations, and submit them to the Senate for its advice and consent."

His conviction of the advantages to our commerce of the reciprocity inaugurated by Congress had so far advanced that he was now prepared, accepting the limited rate of reduction specified by Congress, to make the tentative policy of that body the continuing policy of the Executive administration in respect to commercial treaties.

In his message of 1900 he advanced his views with more positiveness, and we find in the following quotation even a tone of reproach toward the Senate for its inaction: "The failure of action by the Senate at its last session upon the commercial conventions then submitted for its consideration and approval has caused much disappointment to the agricultural and industrial interests of the country, which hoped to profit by their provisions." After advising Congress of the additional conventions which had been signed, he added: "The policy of reciprocity so manifestly rests upon the principles of international equity, and has been so repeatedly approved by the people of the United States, that there ought to be no hesitation in either branch of the Congress in giving to it full effect."

He had been elected by increased majorities for a second term in the fall of 1900. Upon his inauguration on the 4th of March, 1901, in his formal address upon taking anew the oath of office, he once more declared his conviction in these words: "Our diversified productions are increasing in such unprecedented volume as to admonish us of the necessity of still further enlarging our foreign markets by broader commercial relations. For this purpose reciprocal trade arrangements with other nations should in a liberal spirit be carefully cultivated and promoted."

Just before the Presidential journey to the Pacific coast which followed after the inauguration he told me of his purpose to call public attention to reciprocity in his speeches; and he did so.

After all this consultation of the people of the United States his last intimation to me was of an intention to make a stronger demand than ever before in his annual message of next December.

But he did not wait for that official occasion. The international assemblage of industrial and commercial interests at Buffalo in September gave him an earlier opportunity for the most emphatic expressions on the subject ever yet uttered by him. . . .

And this, alas! was the final message of a great and patriotic President to the people whom he loved and who loved him. He saw clearly that the prosperity of our country, standing alone, could not endure. If other countries are impoverished they cannot buy. If increasingly prosperous they increase their purchases. It is the self-interest of every country of vast and varied production that the buying countries should grow in wealth. A nation in poverty is no purchaser, or buys little. A seller must treat his buyer fairly, or he goes elsewhere. It is of Holy Writ that the "liberal soul shall be made fat." It is equally true of the life of nations and of individuals. Witness the present condition of Spain and of Portugal, after many years of an exclusive tariff, in comparison with France and Belgium.

This lesson of international fair-dealing, combined with national industry and energy, is the dead President's last legacy to the United States. Patiently, thoughtfully, he approached his conclusions. After that, no more hesitation, no more doubt. He assumes his proper leadership. Until then he is patient, considerate, receptive. After it he becomes clear, positive, and urgent. Never since its colonial settlement has the country presented a more admirable type of American and Christian citizenship—

> Rich in saving common-sense,
> And, as the greatest only are,
> In his simplicity sublime.

So it has come to pass that we profoundly respect the opinions of him whom we profoundly love. Both his heart and his intellect have conquered us. We trusted him in life; we trust him in his grave. Nay, not in the grave art thou, O beloved President, but warmly nested in the heart of the great republic!

(From *Century,* December, 1901, LXIII, 268-275)

WILLIAM MCKINLEY, "President McKinley's Last Public
Utterance to the People," September 5, 1901

I am glad to be again in the city of Buffalo and exchange greetings
with her people, to whose generous hospitality I am not a stranger and
with whose good will I have been repeatedly and signally honored.
To-day I have additional satisfaction in meeting and giving welcome
to the foreign representatives assembled here, whose presence and
participation in this exposition have contributed in so marked a degree
to its interest and success. To the Commissioners of the Dominion of
Canada and the British colonies, the French colonies, the republics
of Mexico and Central and South America and the commissioners of
Cuba and Puerto Rico, who share with us in this undertaking, we give
the hand of fellowship and felicitate with them upon the triumphs of
art, science, education and manufacture which the old has bequeathed
to the new century. Expositions are the timekeepers of progress. They
record the world's advancement. They stimulate the energy, enterprise and intellect of the people and quicken human genius. They go
into the home. They broaden and brighten the daily life of the people.
They open mighty storehouses of information to the student. Every
exposition, great or small, has helped to some onward step. Comparison of ideas is always educational, and as such instruct the brain and
hand of man. Friendly rivalry follows, which is the spur to industrial
improvement, the inspiration to useful invention and to high endeavor
in all departments of human activity. It exacts a study of the wants,
comforts and even the whims of the people and recognizes the efficiency of high quality and new pieces to win their favor. The quest
for trade is an incentive to men of business to devise, invent, improve
and economize in the cost of production.

Business life, whether among ourselves or with other people, is
ever a sharp struggle for success. It will be none the less so in the
future. Without competition we would be clinging to the clumsy antiquated processes of farming and manufacture and the methods of
business of long ago, and the twentieth would be no further advanced
than the eighteenth century. But though commercial competitors we
are, commercial enemies we must not be.

The Pan-American exposition has done its work thoroughly, presenting in its exhibits evidences of the highest skill and illustrating the progress of the human family in the western hemisphere. This portion of the earth has no cause for humiliation for the part it has performed in the march of civilization. It has not accomplished everything from it. It has simply done its best, and without vanity or boastfulness, and recognizing the manifold achievements of others, it invites the friendly rivalry of all the powers in the peaceful pursuits of trade and commerce, and will co-operate with all in advancing the highest and best interests of humanity.

The wisdom and energy of all the nations are none too great for the world's work. The success of art, science, industry and invention is an international asset and a common glory.

After all, how near one to the other is every part of the world. Modern inventions have brought into close relation widely separated peoples and made them better acquainted. Geographic and political divisions will continue to exist, but distances have been effaced. Swift ships and swift trains are becoming cosmopolitan. They invade fields which a few years ago were impenetrable. The world's products are exchanged as never before, and with increasing transportation facilities come increasing knowledge and larger trade. Prices are fixed with mathematical precision by supply and demand. The world's selling prices are regulated by market and crop reports.

We travel greater distances in a shorter space of time and with more ease than was ever dreamed of by the fathers. Isolation is no longer possible or desirable. The same important news is read, though in different languages, the same day in all Christendom. The telegraph keeps us advised of what is occurring everywhere, and the press foreshadows, with more or less accuracy, the plans and purposes of the nations.

Market prices of products and of securities are hourly known in every commercial mart, and the investments of the people extend beyond their own national boundaries into the remotest parts of the earth. Vast transactions are conducted and international exchanges are made by the tick of the cable. Every event of interest is immediately bulletined. The quick gathering and transmission of news, like rapid transit, are of recent origin and are only made possible by the genius of the inventor and the courage of the investor. It took a special messenger of the Government, with every facility known at the time for rapid travel, 19 days to go from the city of Washington to New Orleans with a message to General Jackson that the war with England had ceased and a treaty of peace had been signed. How different now!

We reached General Miles in Puerto Rico by cable, and he was able, through the military telegraph, to stop his army on the firing line with the message that the United States and Spain had signed a protocol suspending hostilities. We knew almost instantly of the first shots fired at Santiago, and the subsequent surrender of the Spanish forces was known at Washington within less than an hour of its consummation. The first ship of Cervera's fleet had hardly emerged from that historic harbor when the fact was flashed to our capital, and the swift destruction that followed was announced immediately through the wonderful medium of telegraphy.

So accustomed are we to safe and easy communication with distant lands that its temporary interruption, even in ordinary times, results in loss and inconvenience. We shall never forget the days of anxious waiting and awful suspense when no information was permitted to be sent from Peking, and the diplomatic representatives of the nations in China, cut off from all communication, inside and outside of the walled capital, were surrounded by an angry and misguided mob that threatened their lives; nor the joy that filled the world when a single message from the Government of the United States brought through our minister the first news of the safety of the besieged diplomats.

At the beginning of the nineteenth century there was not a mile of steam railroad on the globe. Now there are enough miles to make its circuit many times. Then there was not a line of electric telegraph; now we have a vast mileage traversing all lands and seas. God and man have linked the nations together. No nation can longer be indifferent to any other. And as we are brought more and more in touch with each other the less occasion there is for misunderstandings and the stronger the disposition, when we have differences, to adjust them in the court of arbitration, which is the noblest forum for the settlement of international disputes.

My fellow citizens, trade statistics indicate that this country is in a state of unexampled prosperity. The figures are almost appalling.

They show that we are utilizing our fields and forests and mines and that we are furnishing profitable employment to the millions of workingmen throughout the United States, bringing comfort and happiness to their homes and making it possible to lay by savings for old age and disability. That all the people are participating in this great prosperity is seen in every American community, and shown by the enormous and unprecedented deposits in our savings banks. Our duty is the care and security of these deposits, and their safe investment demands the highest integrity and the best business capacity of those in charge of these depositories of the people's earnings.

We have a vast and intricate business, built up through years of toil and struggle, in which every part of the country has its stake, and will not permit of either neglect or of undue selfishness. No narrow, sordid policy will subserve it. The greatest skill and wisdom on the part of the manufacturers and producers will be required to hold and increase it. Our industrial enterprises which have grown to such great proportions affect the homes and occupations of the people and the welfare of the country. Our capacity to produce has developed so enormously and our products have so multiplied that the problem of more markets requires our urgent and immediate attention. Only a broad and enlightened policy will keep what we have. No other policy will get more. In these times of marvelous business energy and gain we ought to be looking to the future, strengthening the weak places in our industrial and commercial system, that we may be ready for any storm or strain.

By sensible trade arrangements which will not interrupt our home productions we shall extend the outlets for our increasing surplus. A system which provides mutual exchange of commodities, a mutual exchange is manifestly essential to the continued and healthful growth of our export trade. We must not repose in fancied security that we can forever sell everything and buy little or nothing. If such a thing were possible, it would not be best for us or for those with whom we deal. We should take from our customers such of their products as we can use without harm to our industries and labor. Reciprocity is the natural outgrowth of our wonderful industrial development under the domestic policy now firmly established. What we produce beyond our domestic consumption must have a vent abroad. The excess must be relieved through a foreign outlet and we should sell everywhere we can, and thereby make a greater demand for home labor.

The period of exclusiveness is past. The expansion of our trade and commerce is the pressing problem. Commercial wars are unprofitable. A policy of good will and friendly trade relations will prevent reprisals. Reciprocity treaties are in harmony with the times, measures of retaliation are not. If perchance some of our tariffs are no longer needed, for revenue or to encourage and protect our industries at home, why should they not be employed to extend and promote our markets abroad? Then, too, we have inadequate steamship service. New lines of steamers have already been put in commission between the Pacific coast ports of the United States and those on the western coasts of Mexico and Central and South America. These should be followed up with direct steamship lines between the eastern coast of the United States and South American ports. One of the needs of the times is to direct commercial lines from our vast fields of production to the fields of consumption that we have but barely touched. Next in advantage to having the thing to sell is to have the convenience to carry it to the buyer. We must encourage our merchant marine. We must have more ships. They must be under the American flag, built and manned and owned by Americans. These will not only be profitable in a commercial sense; they will be messengers of peace and amity wherever they go. We must build the Isthmian canal, which will unite the two oceans and give a straight line of water communications with the western coasts of Central and South America and Mexico. The construction of a Pacific cable cannot be longer postponed.

In the furthering of these objects of national interest and concern you are performing an important part. This exposition would have touched the heart of that American statesman whose mind was ever alert and thought ever constant for a larger commerce and a truer fraternity of the republics of the new world. His broad American spirit is felt and manifested here. He needs no identification to an assemblage of Americans anywhere, for the name of Blaine is inseparably associated with the Pan-American movement, which finds this practical and substantial expression, and which we all hope will be firmly advanced by the Pan-American congress that assembles this autumn in the capital of

Mexico. The good work will go on. It cannot be stopped. These buildings will disappear; this creation of art and beauty and industry will perish from sight, but its influence will remain to

> Make it live beyond its too short living
> With praises and thanksgiving.

Who can tell the new thoughts that have been awakened, the ambitions fired and the high achievements that will be wrought through this exposition? Gentlemen, let us ever remember that our interest is in concord, not conflict, and that our real eminence rests in the victories of peace, not those of war. We hope that all who are represented here may be moved to higher and nobler effort for their own and the world's good, and that out of this city may come, not only greater commerce and trade, but more essential than these, relations of mutual respect, confidence and friendship which will deepen and endure.

Our earnest prayer is that God will graciously vouchsafe prosperity, happiness and peace to all our neighbors, and like blessings to all the peoples and powers of earth.

(From James D. Richardson, *A Supplement to a Compilation of the Messages and Papers of the Presidents,* Washington, 1902, pp. 292-296)

BROOKS ADAMS, "Reciprocity or the Alternative," 1901

Each year society inclines to accept more unreservedly the theory that war is only an extreme phase of economic competition; and if this postulate be correct, it follows that international competition, if carried far enough, must end in war. An examination of history tends to confirm this view; and thus stated, the doctrine concerns Americans. as the present policy of the United States is to force a struggle for subsistence, of singular intensity, upon Europe.

If a stable economic equilibrium could be maintained, so that not only nations, but individuals, should preserve a fixed relation to each other, war might cease. War persists because civilization is always in movement, the energy and direction of the movement depending largely on the exhaustion of old, and the discovery of new, mines.

In the last century, the iron and coal of Europe not only sufficed for domestic needs, but formed the basis of her wealth by enabling the continent to build up a manufacturing supremacy. That supremacy is already passing away, and in this century European iron and coal seem likely to be largely superseded by American, since the latter are even now sold at a lower price. Clearly, no such fundamental shifting of values as this change would cause could take place without profound social and political disturbances. . . .

Previous to 1890 America had remained chiefly agricultural, buying largely of European manufactures, and paying therefor, in part, in evidences of debt. Her own industries, like those of France under Louis XIV, were then organized on too costly a basis for international competition, and were mostly maintained by a system of bounties under the form of a tariff. After 1870, the economic disturbance in Europe, caused by the rise of Germany, gradually created a stringency in Great Britain; a liquidation assumed proportions which culminated in panic. One method of measuring the pressure to which the United States was subjected during a series of years, and to gauge the change of relations between the eastern and the western continent wrought thereby, is to compare the average yearly payments made on balance by America to foreigners from a date antecedent to the catastrophe of 1893 to the present time.

If three quinquennial periods be taken, beginning with 1887, the first will fall substantially before the crisis of the Baring failure. From 1887 to 1891 the average annual excess of exports over imports amounted to about $44,400,000, a sum certainly not more than sufficient to pay interest due abroad and other like charges. After the failure of the Barings creditors grew pressing, and the balance rose, between 1892 and 1896, to $185,400,000. In 1896 the United States reached the lowest point in her recent history. Her position then somewhat resembled that of France when Colbert adopted his policy of "selling without buying." The cost of production being too high, Americans could not export manufactures; agricultural supplies alone proved insufficient to yield the sum demanded of her; and the country, in that single year, had to part with $78,880,000 in gold. General insolvency seemed imminent. When confronted, in 1667, with stagnating commerce and failing industries, Colbert proclaimed his prohibitive tariff, and finding that this expedient did not correct exchanges, he invaded Holland; but he did not cut the evil he combatted at the root, by reorganizing France. In 1897 the United States followed the precedent set by Colbert, so far as the tariff was concerned; but Americans, suppler than Frenchmen, did not go to war. They adopted a more effective method of routing the foe. They readjusted their entire system of industry and transportation, bringing the cost of production of the chief articles of modern commerce below the European level. No success has ever been more sudden or more startling. Between 1897 and 1901 the average excess of American exports over imports has risen to $510,000,000 yearly. The amount tends to increase, and it tends to increase for excellent reasons. Just now America can undersell Europe in most branches of manufactured iron and steel, besides many minor classes of wares. On the present basis, there seems no reason to doubt that, as time goes on, America will drive Europe more and more from neutral markets, and will, if she makes the effort, flood Europe herself with goods at prices with which Europeans cannot compete.

A moment's consideration will disclose the gravity of the situation. Whatever may have been, or may still be, the extent of America's foreign indebtedness, it is certain that, at the present rate of redemption, it must be soon extinguished. Then the time will come when the whole vast burden of payment for American exports will fall upon the annual earnings of foreign nations, at the moment when those earnings are cut down by the competition of the very goods for which they must pay.

The inversion of all that has heretofore existed has been so sudden and complete that society has somewhat lost its bearings; nevertheless, the feeling of Europe is apprehension, and that feeling is not without rational foundation. Should the movement of the next decade correspond to the movement of the last, Europe will, at its close, stand face to face with ruin. It is safe to assume, therefore, that Europe will not allow present conditions to remain unchanged, any more than France did in 1667, or than America did in 1896.

Three avenues seem open, by which relief may be obtained. First, Europe may reorganize herself upon a scale to correspond with the organization of the United States; but this solution appears doubtful, in view of the decentralization of the continent. Second, the United States may be induced to abandon something of her advantages, and ameliorate the situation of Europe by commercial reciprocity. In other words, the United States may prefer to follow somewhat the same policy which Cobden advocated, as opposed to the policy of Colbert and Napoleon. Lastly, Europe may attack the United States, and attempt to break her down by arms.

In plain English, Europe finds herself in an *impasse*. She is pressed on every hand. Her soil, never rich, has been tilled until its culture costs more than that of newer land. Hence each country must choose between two alternatives: the farmers may be abandoned to their fate, as in the United Kingdom; or they may be protected, as in France and Germany. If the farmers should be abandoned, the military population will disappear, as it has disappeared in Great Britain, and food will have to be bought abroad. If the farmers should be protected, the rest of the country must pay higher for its bread and meat. In either case, the loss will correspond to the sum represented by the inferiority of the European soil, and the higher price it bears, as compared with the soil of Argentina or Nebraska.

Prior to 1897, while Europe still held a substantial monopoly in manufactures, this deterioration of agriculture, if not viewed with pleasure, might be contemplated with equanimity. Not so since 1897, when the industrial revolution in North America has brought European mines to a condition of relative exhaustion, and European workshops to a position of relative inferiority. Assuming that a satisfactory social readjustment offers, just now, insuperable difficulties, Europeans see but one method of obtaining relief, should America retain her tariff: that method is to develop regions abroad containing mines capable of vying with those of Alabama, Pennsylvania, and Lake Superior. And it is precisely here that Europe finds herself propelled toward a collision with the United States, because the United States, for her own protection, has devised a mechanism which holds her rival as in a vise.

America's attack is based not only on her superior resources and her more perfect administration, but on her tariff. To make their gigantic industrial system lucrative, Americans have comprehended that it must be worked at the highest velocity and at its full capacity, and they have taken their measures accordingly. To guard against a check they rely on a practically prohibitive tariff, by which they hope to maintain the home market at a reasonable level; and with the profit thus obtained they expect to make good any loss which may accrue from forcing their surplus upon foreigners at prices with which these cannot cope. No wonder the European regards America as a dangerous and relentless foe; and the fact that Europe has forced on America these measures as a means of self-defense signifies nothing. The European sees in America a competitor who, while refusing to buy, throws her wares on every market, and who, while she drives the peasant from his land, reduces the profits of industry which support the wage-earners of the town. Most ominous of all, he marks a rapidly growing power, which, while it undersells his mines, closes to him every region of the wide earth where he might find minerals adapted to his needs. Lying like a colossus across the western continent, with her ports on either ocean, with China opposite and South America at her feet, the United States bars European expansion. South America and China are held to be the only accessible regions which certainly contain the iron, coal, and copper which Europe seeks; and the United States is determined that, if she can prevent it, South America and China shall not be used as bases for hostile competition. Regarding South America her declarations are explicit, and during the last 12 months her actions in Asia have spoken more emphatically than words.

Moreover, the German considers the theory of the "open door" a mockery. The German avers that no man knows so well as the American that China can never be developed until it is administered by western methods, and that it is for this reason that America opposes partition. To make Asia pay, the country must be handled as a whole, —as America is handled, though not perhaps on so extensive a scale. At all events, in each province the mining, transportation, manufactures, police, and taxation must be controlled by Europeans. To attempt to turn Shansi into a Pennsylvania under Chinese rule would mean ruin.

Thus the continent of Europe finds itself pressed somewhat as

Colbert found France pressed in 1667, and accordingly Europeans are restive. Evidently, unless all human experience is at fault, that restiveness will grow. Men cannot foresee the future,—they can only reason about it by reference to the past; and as they can never know all the forces in operation, their inferences must contain more or less of error. For example, this year competition appears to be approaching, in intensity, the point of danger; and yet next year an abundant supply of gold may raise prices, and thereby allay friction for an indefinite period. Yet, speaking generally and without limit of time, the great question of American economic supremacy remains to be settled; and as long as Europe continues armed that question will not be settled peacefully upon America's own terms as America is now organized. There must be compromise or war, or else America must be so strong that war is deemed too hazardous to be attempted.

A compromise is a bargain, each side giving as little as it can; but doubtless the United States could make arrangements which would meet the emergency. The policy of England has always been to make such arrangements; and in this she has differed from France. Free trade as an economic dogma, applicable to all conditions of national life, has been exploded; but free trade as a form of insurance against hostile coalitions has worked well. England has found free trade cheaper than to arm; she would certainly find it more advantageous than to fight. No coalition has ever been formed against Great Britain since she became great; for evidently no one will plunge into hostilities, where little is to be made by war, and much by peace. Prussia has long maintained great armaments, and has sometimes made concessions, and sometimes used force. On the whole, Prussia has fared better than any other Continental state. Policy is a matter of judgment.

Americans are apt to reckon on their geographical position as in itself an insurance against war risks, on the principle that, like the tortoise, they are invulnerable if they withdraw within their shell. Such was the case formerly, but is not the case now. On the contrary, in European eyes, America offers the fairest prize to plunder that has been known since the sack of Rome, and according to European standards, she is almost as unprotected as was Holland before Louis XIV.

First of all, America is valuable not only for what she has herself, but for what she keeps from others; for even without her islands, the United States now closes South America and China. Were she defeated, these two vast territories would lie open to division. But more than this, Continental Europeans apprehend that were the United States crushed on the sea, were her islands taken from her, were she shut up within her own borders, all the rest of the world, save the British Empire, would fall to them, and that they might exclude American products at their will. They believe that American society would not stand the strain of the dislocation of the industrial system incident to the interruption of exports, and that disturbances would ensue which would remove all fear of American supremacy. Also, Continental statesmen are not lacking who conceive that England might see more profit in helping to divide the lion's skin than in binding up his wounds. Nor must it ever be forgotten that, with Great Britain, the success of the European or the American continent is only a choice of evils. America is her most dangerous competitor save Germany and Russia. Great Britain, therefore, at present, holds to America, as the lesser peril; but should, at a given moment, the weight in the other scale of the balance preponderate, England would shift to the side of our antagonist.

Assuming, for the moment, for the sake of argument, that the United States is determined to yield nothing, but is resolved to push all her advantages to the uttermost, it is clear that an attack upon her would be profitable, if it could be made with reasonable hope of success. Europe believes that it could be made with such hope, provided a coalition could be opportunely formed. In this Europeans may be wrong; but they judge after their own standards, and possibly they may be right.

America has an army of less than 100,000 men, with a short supply of officers, and no reserves either of soldiers or of material. At the mere rumor of war 100,000 men would have to leave the country to garrison Cuba, Porto Rico, the canal, the Philippines, and Hawaii. More ought to go, if more could be obtained. But to send 100,000 men abroad would strip the Union bare. Even the ports would be defended by militia, and no reinforcements would be at hand to supply the waste in the tropics. Such garrisons could hardly stand against the overwhelming mass of troops which could be concentrated against them.

The navy is even feebler, in proportion to the task which would be required of it. The United States has 520,000 tons of warships, built or building. France and Germany have 1,162,000, and France, Germany, and Russia have 1,731,000.

Americans, furthermore, are disposed to assume that no coalition could ever be formed against them. Judging by the past, nothing can be more certain than that coalitions both can and will be formed against them, if they so behave as to make such ventures worth the cost and risk. Combinations always have been made, under such conditions, and probably always will continue to be made. To be opulent, unarmed, and aggressive is to put a premium upon them. An arrangement of this character was, in fact, contemplated in 1898, and is generally believed to have been abandoned only through uncertainty as to the neutrality of England.

Suppose an alliance of two or more powers, of which France were to be one: they would possess an admirable base in the West Indies, in Martinique or Guadeloupe, and also convenient bases in Asia. No station on the whole Asiatic coast is more commanding than Port Arthur, held by Russia. Fleets, therefore, of any size could be concentrated and supplied close to the seat of war, and Europeans compute that ships could be concentrated against us at the least in the ratio of two to one.

Our rivals believe that a couple of defeats secured by overwhelming numbers would settle the war; for ironclads cannot be built in less than two or three years, and they calculate that two or three years of isolation, resulting from the loss of control of the sea, would produce enough domestic unrest to enforce acceptance of their future safety.

Such possibilities have not yet been maturely considered in the United States, because the change in the position occupied by the country is recent. Men do not immediately divest themselves of their old prejudices. Nevertheless, Americans are inclined to believe, and with reason, that their country is becoming the modern seat of empire. If this be so, they must accept the dangers and the cost of greatness with its advantages. All situations have their drawbacks.

From 1815 to the Boer war England claimed to be the financial capital of the world, and that claim was admitted. England, consequently, paid heavily to insure herself against attack. She not only maintained a navy supposed to be equal to that of any combination which could probably be formed against her, but, adopting free trade, she bought from all. France proceeded on the opposite theory; and yet, although France has kept up vast armies, she has been thrice disastrously defeated, twice actually conquered, and has never attained her end.

If a country would live in peace, experience has demonstrated that she must not be too grasping; for excessive greed makes her overthrow a benefit to all, and competitors act accordingly. On the other hand, certain races have felt themselves adapted to win victory in battle, and have prospered; if the American people, after due deliberation, feel aggression to be for their best interest, there is little to be urged by way of precedent against the logic of their decision.

Men inclining to this attitude can point to history, and insist that no radical readjustment of the world's economic equilibrium has ever been unaccompanied by war; and that if war must come, the United States may well face it now. To abandon any advantage would be weakness. The United States is young, strong, rich, and energetic, with an enormous military population. No permanent tranquility can be hoped for until her supremacy is acknowledged: therefore the course which will enforce that acknowledgement soonest is the cheapest. America is as likely now as she will ever be to emerge victorious from any conflict into which she may enter.

To such reasoning it might be objected that war has proved too uncertain to be hazarded save in extremity, and the failure of the British speculation in the Transvaal might be cited as a warning. But such an argument would savor of an expression of personal opinion on a question of expediency, and this article is confined to an attempt to draw deductions as to fixed social laws from the facts of history.

No one can deny that certain nations have made war profitable: therefore profitable wars will probably occur in the future. Nevertheless, such nations have succeeded because they were military nations; that is to say, because they made war a business, and waged it better and cheaper than their rivals. In other words, they devoted their energies to fighting, and maintained fleets and armies as we maintain railroads and factories. To conduct hostilities as amateurs is futile, as the English have discovered.

If Americans are determined to reject reciprocity in all its forms, to insist on their advantages, to concede nothing to the adversary; if, having driven in the knife, they mean to turn it in the wound, they should recognize that they are provoking reprisals in every form, and accept the situation with its limitations. To carry out an aggressive policy in some security, the United States needs 300,000 trained men whom she can put in the field in 20 days, with an ample reserve of officers and of material. She needs well-fortified coasts and colonies, and an effective transport service. More especially, she needs a navy. Judging by the example of England, who has always done her best to make her friendship of value, 100 battleships and armored cruisers, equipped and ready for sea, would hardly suffice.

In a word, the experience of ages has demonstrated that alternatives are presented to aspiring nations in regard to the payment they will make for their prize. The one is the alternative of Cobden, the other that of Colbert. There is no middle course. Destruction has awaited the gambler who backs his luck; the braggart who would be at once rich, aggressive, and unarmed. Such a man or such a nation puts a premium on spoliation. It is only necessary to reflect upon the fate of France in 1870, to accept this inference as true. America enjoys no immunity from natural laws. She can pay for what she takes, or she can fight for it, but she cannot have the earth for nothing. Sooner or later the inexorable tribute will be exacted from her as it has been exacted from every predominant community, from the days of the grandeur of Babylon to those of the glory of London; for, since time began, no race has won for itself supremacy without paying a price in gold or blood to other races as ambitious and almost as powerful as itself.

(From *The Atlantic Monthly,* August, 1901, LXXXVIII, 145-155)

MARCUS A. HANNA, "Remarks on Ship Subsidy Bill," 1902

My conclusion, after considering this whole question from an economic standpoint, as far as my personal investigation has gone and as far as I been able to obtain information, is that this measure is purely an attempt to equalize conditions. All that we of the United States want in this contest for the transportation of the world's goods is a fair show and an equal chance, and I might answer the whole argument made by the Senator from Georgia by repeating the question of the Senator from Kansas yesterday: "If what you say is true, why have we not the ships?" Why have we not? Why does not capital seek that sort of investment if we can build and operate ships as cheaply in this country as our competitors can? The answer to it is that we can not, and the result of it is we have not the ships.

No man in the United States is so well qualified to speak upon this question from experience and knowledge as is the chairman of the Committee on Commerce, and he has never submitted a proposition to the Congress of the United States that was not founded upon the best economic and business principles and in the interest of the development of this country. He has not studied this situation with any idea of making political capital from it. He has studied it not only from the position of an enthusiast, but as a past master in the great question of transportation which, to my mind, Mr. President, stands foremost among the great problems yet unsolved before the American people and the people of every other country.

The growth and development of the United States have absorbed not only the interest but the capital of this country up to recent years, when it has come to pass that the United States is no longer a little nation, but that gradually is becoming the financial center of the world, and we begin to realize that in order to be prosperous and grow bigger we must find employment for capital as well as labor. That is the proposition which confronts us to-day in the industrial part of this question.

The chairman stated in his explanation of the bill that under its provisions, should it become a law, it was reasonable to expect that within the limit of five years we would have constructed and under construction $50,000,000 worth of shipping in the United States. . . .

This brings me to another question. I am in favor . . . of building up the Navy. I am in sympathy with that policy because I know that every ship we build brings that much more physical protection to us and our commerce. But, Mr. President, it strikes me as being almost a ridiculous proposition to talk of putting millions of dollars into our Navy and adding millions more for the construction of an isthmian canal, for what? For the use of the merchant marine and navies of other countries. We have nothing on the high seas to protect except our coastwise ships, and they can easily find shelter behind the guns of our fortifications. When the Stars and Stripes are never seen hardly in any port of the world except on naval men-of-war, is not this a commentary upon a policy that would hesitate in the expenditure of a little money to construct, at the same time we are building our Navy, a merchant marine commensurate with our power and our necessity?

Everyone knows that we are now engaged in a hand-to-hand contest with foreign nations to secure the commerce of the Orient. We have been foremost and steadfast in our policy to secure the markets of China and hold them as an open door, and with the control of our own archipelago, the Philippines, in a short time we shall be able to put there our own conditions of trade. That is the key of the Orient: and when it has become a naval station, surrounded by all the protection that a maritime fleet would need, it becomes a factor in all commercial conditions of the Orient.

It is the purpose to establish new lines under the postal system, from which the United States Government derives a revenue equal at the present day to over $3,000,000 per annum. It is the purpose of the bill to establish a line to South America. On the east side, the Atlantic coast, of South America we have an enormous trade, and with the exception of that carried by tramp steamers every pound of stuff goes to Liverpool or Hamburg and from thence to South America. Every time it is handled or transferred it pays a cost for doing that to somebody, and in the transaction of that business, the storage and the distribution, the financial part of it comes through the machinery of a foreign government and pays a tribute to them equal to a satisfactory profit on every particle of manufactured goods that we export.

There is no denying that proposition, Mr. President. We can not measure the benefits except by the aid of those who know the conditions and who are competent to figure from the transactions of business just what the result will be. But we do know that England gained her supremacy in the markets of the world and upon the high seas, the expansion of her trade to every part of the world, by pursuing steadily the policy of establishing direct communication. Personal contact is what brings results. When we place New York and Buenos Aires and Rio de Janeiro in weekly or semiweekly contact by a line of mail steamers, we will open up an avenue for trade yet unknown, because untried.

The same principle, Mr. President, will apply to every other route proposed in this bill. It is a well-known fact that England, Germany and France are to-day energetically at work to put in the connecting link between the Pacific and the Orient, making propositions and agreeing to the terms of anybody on this side to place in connection with their railroad companies and transportation lines that connecting link between San Francisco and Seattle and China, Manila, and Japan. They are old hands at this business. They have been doing it for a century.

Nothing has disturbed the equilibrium of the shipowner of England and Germany so much as has this bill, which has been discussed openly and publicly upon the floors of Congress for the last two or three years. If I wanted to fortify argument by newspaper articles or articles from magazines or interviews I could fill pages of the RECORD with such articles written in England and Germany, and I could furnish testimony that would show that a concrete effort has been persistently made from the very beginning of the discussion two years ago, by all the influences that could be brought to bear upon Congress, to defeat this measure. I could furnish evidence from the statements of the presidents themselves of some of the largest steamer lines in England that if this new American policy, so mentioned, should be a success, in 50 years the United States would lead the world in ocean transportation.

Now, with reference to the investment of capital, Mr. President. American capital will go wherever it can find a proper return; it does not make any difference upon which side of the Atlantic Ocean that place is. I said a moment ago that we were a creditor instead of a debtor nation. Yet there are millions of American capital now lying in investments abroad that are paying better returns to that capital than it can earn here under the conditions of to-day. That may be one reason why Mr. Morgan or any other capitalist may see fit to invest his money in foreign ships rather than in American ships, because it can be demonstrated as an absolute fact that to put capital into a large steamer in a foreign service for doing exactly what the others are doing and have to do would make a certain loss. And why? Because as has been claimed and as is true, the cost of the investment is more, the cost of operation is more, and because they go into direct competition with subsidized mail ships all over the world.

The chairman of the committee cited the other day in his explanation the amount of subsidies paid by the great nations—Germany, the last to embark in the enterprise, is to-day exercising the best judgment, increasing wherever a new line can be found that will bring her in contact with new markets, and to-day she is negotiating to put two lines not under a mail subsidy contract with the United States, but two lines from the Pacific coast to the Orient, under subsidies from Germany. France has already adopted the generous subsidy plan of subsidizing, as we propose to do, the whole merchant marine owned in that country, and proposes to go further and to offer extraordinary inducements for the investment of capital in that kind of transportation which she finds she must have in order to compete with Germany and England. . . .

It is a well-known fact, Mr. President, that nearly every cotton mill in the South, all of which have been very prosperous in the last few years, finds its market in northern China, and when the opportunity was offered and the rate of freight and contract for delivery could be made which transported those goods from the side track of the mills and delivered them into the warehouses at Hongkong or Yokohama, that trade began to grow and grow, and is to-day the most profitable branch of any manufacturing industry which the Southern States have.

I wish that those States might be spotted over with cotton mills, so that the cotton growers and their laborers, who are looking for work, may seize the opportunity when it comes.

I want them to have all possible opportunities, but this question of the connecting link between the producer and the consumer must solve that proposition, and not theorizing as to what it is good policy to do, whether you subsidize a ship or whether you do not. Give them the opportunity for this contact. Bring businessmen together, the purchaser and the man who has the goods to sell, and they will find a way to exchange commodities or to sell their products. None of us would be willing to admit that the American merchant or the American manufacturer could be outdone in competition in the world's markets by those of any other nation if you place him on an equality with them. . . .

But I do want to urge upon this Senate and this Congress as a business proposition, in addition to a patriotic one, not to let this opportunity, which may never again return under like conditions, pass by. Because, Mr. President, if we do not the other fellow will take advantage of this new era in the opening up and the development of the markets of the Orient, when the spirit of trade and the expansion of commerce is enlivening all the world; and when our people have the ability and the facility to accomplish all that could be asked or expected of them, we should stand ready, as the representatives of the American people and of American progress, to step in and do that which they can not do, unless they have the tools with which to do it. That one missing link is the only thing.

(From *The Congressional Record,* March 6, 1902)

JOHN FOORD, "The Russian Advance Across Asia," 1904

Let me explain for a little how it comes that the characteristic Russian policy applied to Eastern Asia should have for the United States a very close interest indeed. The policy of this country in regard to its position and future as a Pacific Power has been, so far, marked by a degree of vigor and directness comparable only to its attitude toward all questions involving the application or interpretation of the Monroe Doctrine. If the external policy of our Government has anywhere been open to the charge of aggressiveness it has been in relation to our interests as the custodians of the gateway of the Pacific; the apology for planting our flag over non-contiguous territory has been that it was virtually essential to our future greatness and prosperity that we should occupy a place of preponderant authority and influence in the great Pacific area, in and around which is massed half the human race. The Alaskan purchase was dictated by a desire to grasp the opportunity to become the foremost of Pacific Powers; the acquisition of Hawaii was a testimony to the necessity of excluding foreign control from a commanding position in mid-Pacific; the taking of the Philippines was justified on the ground that we needed an emporium of trade and a place of arms to be ready against the time when other Powers might be moved to dispute the right of the United States to enjoy equality of commercial opportunity in the great markets of Eastern Asia. We have made the construction of a canal across the Isthmus of Panama a national enterprise, primarily because it was needed to enable all sections of our country to have the full benefit of the present and future profit of the commerce of the Pacific. . . .

If the extension of the influence of the United States has been anywhere pursued in obedience to the call of "manifest destiny," it has been on and around the Pacific Ocean. If there be one point more than another where a check to our influence would dwarf the role which this republic is fitted to play on the stage of history it would be here. There can be no shutting our eyes to the fact that the consummation of the policy which has been deliberately pursued by Russia in Eastern Asia must nullify the advantages we possess on the Pacific, and render meaningless every effort we have made to confirm our influence as the greatest of Pacific Powers. The natural outcome of that policy could be nothing less than the partition of the most populous of empires and the richest of all the unexploited regions of the earth among the Great Powers of Europe, to the destruction of all the rights of trade which we have acquired by treaty with that empire, and to the exclusion for all time of our influence and enterprise from the gigantic and immensely profitable undertaking of equipping China with the appliances and supplying it with the products of modern civilization.

(From *Journal of the American Asiatic Association,* April, 1904, IV, 72-77)

QUADRANGLE PAPERBACKS

History

Frederick Lewis Allen. *The Lords of Creation.* QP35
Lewis Atherton. *Main Street on the Middle Border.* QP36
Thomas A. Bailey. *Woodrow Wilson and the Lost Peace.* QP1
Thomas A. Bailey. *Woodrow Wilson and the Great Betrayal.* QP2
Charles A. Beard. *The Idea of National Interest.* QP27
Carl L. Becker. *Everyman His Own Historian.* QP33
Ray A. Billington. *The Protestant Crusade.* QP12
John Chamberlain. *Farewell to Reform.* QP19
Chester McArthur Destler. *American Radicalism, 1865-1901.* QP30
Elisha P. Douglass. *Rebels and Democrats.* QP26
Herman Finer. *Road to Reaction.* QP5
Felix Frankfurter. *The Commerce Clause.* QP16
Lloyd C. Gardner. *A Different Frontier.* QP32
Ray Ginger. *Altgeld's America.* QP21
Louis Joughin and Edmund M. Morgan. *The Legacy of Sacco and Vanzetti.* QP7
Edward Chase Kirkland. *Dream and Thought in the Business Community, 1860-1900.* QP11
Adrienne Koch. *The Philosophy of Thomas Jefferson.* QP17
Walter LaFeber. *John Quincy Adams and American Continental Empire.* QP23
David E. Lilienthal. *TVA: Democracy on the March.* QP28
Arthur S. Link. *Wilson the Diplomatist.* QP18
Huey P. Long. *Every Man a King.* QP8
Gene M. Lyons. *America: Purpose and Power.* QP24
Jackson Turner Main. *The Antifederalists.* QP14
Ernest R. May. *The World War and American Isolation, 1914-1917.* QP29
Henry F. May. *The End of American Innocence.* QP9
George E. Mowry. *The California Progressives.* QP6
Frank L. Owsley. *Plain Folk of the Old South.* QP22
David Graham Phillips. *The Treason of the Senate.* QP20
Julius W. Pratt. *Expansionists of 1898.* QP15
Richard W. Van Alstyne. *The Rising American Empire.* QP25
Willard M. Wallace. *Appeal to Arms.* QP10
Norman Ware. *The Industrial Worker, 1840-1860.* QP13
Albert K. Weinberg. *Manifest Destiny.* QP3
Bernard A. Weisberger. *They Gathered at the River.* QP37
Bell I. Wiley. *The Plain People of the Confederacy.* QP4
William Appleman Williams. *The Contours of American History.* QP34
Esmond Wright. *Causes and Consequences of the American Revolution.* QP31

Philosophy

James M. Edie. *An Invitation to Phenomenology.* QP103
George L. Kline. *European Philosophy Today.* QP102
Pierre Thévenaz. *What Is Phenomenology?* QP101

Social Science

George and Eunice Grier. *Equality and Beyond.* QP204
David Mitrany. *A Working Peace System.* QP205
Martin Oppenheimer and George Lakey. *A Manual for Direct Action.* QP202
Erwin A. Salk. *A Layman's Guide to Negro History.* QP206
Egon Schwelb. *Human Rights and the International Community.* QP203
Clarence Senior. *The Puerto Ricans.* QP201